CONT

A FRIENDLY OFFER?

01

Q Nick doesn't like fore and aft mooring buoys. He finds them difficult to pick up and, once secured, they seem to put very heavy loads on the mooring lines, particularly with the tidal stream from astern and a crosswind. Having read in the sailing directions that the only mooring option in Chausey Sound was between fore and aft buoys, he was thinking about giving up the plan for an overnight visit to the islands southeast of Jersey. His crew had heard that this was a magical place though, and persuaded him that, as it was neap tides and no more than a Force 4-5 forecast, it would be a shame to pass them by.

As it turned out, there was plenty of room on the moorings and, with the help of smart work from the crew, Nick picked up a suitable pair of buoys without a problem. The wind had been light when they arrived and dropped to nothing overnight so his worry about strain on the deck cleats and mooring lines was ill-founded.

The following day he planned to leave through the shallow northern end of the Sound, which meant waiting until mid-afternoon for sufficient rise of tide and a favourable stream. By lunch the wind had built to the promised Force 4-5 from the northeast, right abeam, and the heavy warp risers from the buoys were leading to windward at quite a shallow angle.

WIND

Risers to mooring buoys blocking windward side approach

After lunch an elderly couple onboard a French yacht, slightly smaller than Nick's, were having considerable difficulty mooring to a pair of buoys across the Sound. They made good approaches but just didn't have the strength or agility to get their warps onto the buoys before the wind blew them out of reach. After their fourth unsuccessful attempt, Nick took pity on them. He hailed them, explained that he was planning to leave in a couple of hours and asked if they would like to come alongside.

His offer was accepted without hesitation and with obvious relief. The Frenchman put plenty of fenders over his starboard side and lined up to come alongside Nick's port side. It was soon apparent that he wasn't going to make it as the cable from the aft buoy was blocking his approach. The Frenchman also spotted the problem and hauled off to port, asking if he could come alongside Nick's starboard side instead.

At this point, Nick silently curses himself for his friendly offer but he can hardly withdraw it. If the Frenchman comes alongside to leeward it presents Nick with a devil of a job to leave. He'll have 18 knots of wind blowing him onto his new neighbour, the risers from the buoys blocking his route out ahead and stern and no appreciable tidal stream to help lift him clear.

At least his French and the Frenchman's English are good enough to allow reasonable communication. As long as he keeps things simple, he should be able to come up with a sensible solution.

What would you do?

One solution might be to allow the Frenchman to come alongside to leeward and, once he has secured, to wind the boats so that Nick finishes up on the leeward side. It would need many metres of rope and much heaving and hauling. It could put a considerable strain on the bilingual communication but it would be possible.

A more elegant solution would be to invite the Frenchman to stop his boat parallel to Nick's but far enough upwind to clear the buoy risers on the approach, then let the wind bring him alongside, more or less parallel. There is a risk that the Frenchman will get the manoeuvre slightly wrong and the bow or stern will pay off first, resulting in a rather ugly contact between Nick's topsides and a sharp corner of the French boat.

However Nick has watched the Frenchman's boat-handling and has no reason to doubt his ability – it is only his lack of agility and brawn that has prevented him from picking up his own pair of buoys. Given the French skipper's agreement and plenty of well-placed fenders on both boats, it should be worth a try.

DON'T SPILL THE CREW

02

Q The only really comfortable sea berth in Peter and Alice's boat is the starboard saloon berth. Peter had always believed that this was why north-bound cross-Channel passages always seemed easier than south-bound. The wind is usually westerly so the off-watch crew simply flops into the bunk without the need to rig and then climb over a lee cloth, and Peter always slept better knowing that he didn't have to negotiate a lee cloth to come on deck in a hurry. Tonight though, its comfort causes a dilemma.

Peter and Alice cast off and headed north back across the Channel just before dark. With the wind just slightly north of west, they would be close-hauled for at least the first few hours to clear the shipping channels. When Peter came on deck to take over the watch at midnight, a line of east-bound ships was already visible ahead. An hour later, he realised a trawler was weaving to and fro about half a mile ahead with a mean course more or less parallel to their own but with frequent heading alterations. About three miles off their port bow, the lights of a ship were closing on a steady bearing. There were several other lights visible but none looked likely to pass close.

As the stand-on vessel he was obliged to maintain his course and speed until it became apparent that the approaching ship wasn't taking appropriate action to keep clear. He decided to keep going until the ship had closed to about a mile. If she was still holding her course and speed and closing on a steady bearing, then he had a problem.

Peter considers his options. If he bears away onto a parallel course, he'll be sailing dead downwind and giving away valuable ground to leeward, which goes against his instincts as a seaman. Also, with the relative speed of his own boat and the ship reduced, it's going to be a tediously long time before he can resume his northerly course. To turn to port he would have to tack, which would tip Alice out of her bunk and he didn't want to wake her.

Perhaps he could just pinch a little? That would cut his speed and allow the ship to pass ahead. Or he could hold his course and ease the mainsheet, which would have much the same effect. Tacking would definitely be a bad idea – there is, he remembers, something in the COLREGS that advises against an alteration to port by the stand-on vessel – but neither does he want to bear away.

The ship is now, he judged, just under a mile away. Her bearing remains obstinately steady and the aspect of her lights is exactly the same as when he had first sighted her. Time for action.

What would you do?

A Peter has left things a little late, at this stage there really is no elegant solution. About 15 minutes earlier, when it was becoming apparent that he might have to alter course, he could have gone below and put Alice's lee cloth in place, leaving all his options open and keeping Alice asleep in her bunk. Now it's too late for that. He needs to stay on deck to keep a close eye on the ship and do something to get out of harm's way.

He is about 70 per cent right in his memory of COLREGS Rule 17, regarding action by the stand-on vessel. In fact, the 'don't turn to port' advice applies to power driven vessels but, in this situation, it's good advice for Peter too.

Apart from spilling the crew, there are two disadvantages of a turn to port. If the ship manoeuvres to keep clear, her most likely action will be a turn to starboard to duck Peter's stern. If Peter turns to port at the same time, the two manoeuvres could cancel each other out and increase the risk of collision. Also, as closing speed will have increased, the time available for evasive action is reduced.

Slowing down has its attractions, but also its disadvantages. It will not be immediately apparent to the ship that the yacht has taken avoiding action because there will be no instant change of aspect. And, if Peter sails very slowly, he will have little chance of turning quickly if the ship does something unexpected.

The safest initial action for Peter is to turn directly away from the ship, which will be immediately apparent to the ship's watchkeeper. This probably means a gybe and a startled Alice, but better that than both of them taking a long, cold swim. If the ship maintains her course and speed, her lights will very soon start to draw right and it should be safe for Peter to turn full circle back to his original course and pass clear astern of the ship.

What about the trawler? She doesn't really affect the issue. Peter just has to keep an eye on her to make sure that she doesn't take avoiding action for the ship that makes her a collision hazard too.

Dick hardly seemed to have been asleep for five minutes when he heard James calling him: 'Could you come on deck, please? It's thick fog and I think I can hear engines.'

Dick had been expecting the fog. The forecast had warned of fog patches towards dawn and before he handed over the watch to James, the stars in the western sky had disappeared. He was in the cockpit in less than half a minute.

It certainly was foggy, the masthead light was surrounded in bright halo and there was no sign of anything else at all. All the stars had gone, it was still pitch-dark and there was no sign of a horizon in any direction. James had been absolutely right about the engine noise, it was faint but sounded just like a medium-speed diesel, possibly a fishing boat.

The light breeze was from the starboard beam and the GPS showed a speed over the ground of about three knots.

'Sorry to wake you,' said James, 'but I'm worried about being able to hear a ship when I can't see it. It hasn't been there for long and it sounds to me as if it's on our starboard beam. Have you any idea what the visibility is?'

'Certainly less than a mile, probably less than half a mile,' Dick replied. 'With nothing in sight, it's always difficult to tell, but I certainly wouldn't expect to hear another boat's engine much more than half a mile away. That really is all we have to go on.'

'Should we be sounding a fog signal?' asked James.

'Waste of time,' Dick replied. 'The watchkeeper in that boat is almost certainly inside the wheelhouse, so there isn't a hope of him hearing us – and he isn't making any fog signal himself.'

'Should we clip on our safety harnesses?' asked James.

'No,' said Dick. 'Never clip on in fog. If we have a collision the last thing we want is to be tied onto a sinking boat.'

'How about starting the engine?' suggested James. 'Then, if something appears out of the fog at close range, at least we'll have better manoeuvrability to take last-minute avoiding action.' Dick didn't like to sound negative to his nervous young crew but he knew that he did not want the engine started. 'Better not,' he said. 'If we start the engine we won't be able to hear anything approaching. As long as we can hear him, we'll have a good idea whether he's getting closer and whether or not his bearing is changing.'

James fell silent but Dick could see in the glow of the compass light that he wasn't happy with the situation.

Put yourself in the skipper's position.

What would you do?

Dick seems to be getting things about half-right and half-wrong. His estimate of visibility is spot on, based on the sound of the other boat's engine. The halo of reflection from water droplets around the navigation light confirms that visibility is very poor.

As far as the fog signal is concerned, it's unfortunate that he is probably correct in his view of the likelihood of anyone in an enclosed bridge or wheelhouse hearing it. But what if there is another yacht around and her skipper also thinks that fog signals are a waste of time? Probably better to make fog signals, but not to count on them being heard by an approaching ship or fishing vessel.

Dick's reasoning about safety harnesses in fog has some justification, although the chances of going overboard are no less than in good visibility. Clipping on in the cockpit in calm weather seems overly cautious, but working on deck in the dark, use a harness everytime, whatever the visibility. There has been no mention of lifejackets and thick fog is one occasion on which it makes sense for everyone to wear a lifejacket.

It's true that running the engine is likely to be more of a hindrance than a help, but it is worth giving it a short run to make sure that it is ready to start at a moment's notice. His assumption that he will be able to detect change of bearing of engine noise may be optimistic – it is sometimes impossible to be sure of the direction of sound in fog. You can, however, make a reasonable estimate of whether a noise is getting closer or moving further away and at very close range you can hear the bow wave as well as the engine. It is certainly worth making the best possible use of your ears, and your own engine will mask a great deal of useful information.

Another important point that hasn't been mentioned is the use of the radar reflector, which needs to be hoisted if it is not permanently mounted.

Some skippers advocate broadcasting their position, course and speed on VHF radio at low power if they hear a ship approaching. Its effectiveness is debatable, better to rely on the best possible visual and audio lookout. Or better still, fit radar.

THE RUSH HOUR

04

Q Nick had been furious with himself when the engine had failed to start. It was, he knew, entirely his own fault, forgetting to isolate the engine battery the previous evening, then running the heater for four hours and weighing anchor in the morning with the electric windlass. No wonder there wasn't enough left in the poor old batteries to coax the engine into life when they reached the river entrance.

It was five miles upstream to his mooring. Normally, returning with the crowd of weekenders heading homewards, he would have motored. Luckily the wind was no more than a sea breeze so it was a relatively simple reach or run all the way and he had begun to enjoy the peace and quiet of sailing up-river. True, there was a continuous stream of boats under engine overtaking him, their crews blissfully unaware that he could listen to every word of their conversations as they shouted to each other to make themselves heard above the noise of their own engines.

With a little over a mile to go he encountered his first real problem. A closely packed fleet of dinghies appeared round the corner, beating down towards him. It was the local sailing club's Sunday evening race and they had a really good turn out, there must have been at least thirty of them.

'Don't worry Dad,' said Nick's daughter Penny who was keeping a close eye on the situation. 'They'll be turning upriver at that yellow mark about 180 metres ahead of us. Then we'll be going in the same direction and they go faster than us so we'll soon be in clear water again.'

Nick knew she was right, the trouble was that he would be past their windward mark several minutes before they reached it. He was on a very broad reach on port tack so he would have to keep out of the way of every boat in the fleet.

He looked astern, no gaps in the convoy of cruising boats motoring upriver so turning round and tacking through that lot in his 40-footer would be even worse than trying to thread his way through the dinghy fleet. He couldn't anchor in that reach of the river, the bottom was rock so he would either drag or plant his anchor irretrievably into a fissure. There wasn't even a mooring buoy he could hang onto for ten minutes.

He needed to slow down. He eased the mainsheet, but the boom went hard against the shroud and the speed actually increased by a fraction of a knot. The headsail was already partly blanketed behind the main and doing very little. He needed to find a way of stopping, or at least cutting his speed from the five knots he was currently making to about two, that would see the dinghy fleet round their mark and heading back up river before he reached them.

'What should we do Dad?' asked Penny expectantly. 'Do you want me to get the main down?'

What would you do?

Lowering the main would probably not be a good idea. It would certainly be bad for the sail to drag it down against the shrouds and it is quite likely that it would jam, still part hoisted, just adding to the problem.

Better to sheet the main as hard as possible and roll up or lower the headsail. He should still have good steerage way but with such little effective area for the wind to work on the speed should be very slow.

If that isn't quite enough to avoid the racers he is just going to have to keep well over to one side of the river and shout to any approaching dinghy that's foolish enough to try to enforce the rules for meeting sailing boats that he is very sorry but he can't get out of their way. Chances are that he will have no problem with the boats at the front of the fleet. The back markers may well be more of a problem and one or two of them will no doubt trot out that horrid little phrase 'I am racing, you know.'

The only possible answer is 'I'm very sorry, you were going so slowly I thought you were just out for an evening's potter down the river.'

Q Howard and Mary always enjoy the two-week summer cruise with their family and they make a strong team. The two boys spend more of their university terms on the rugby field than attending lectures, their daughter married a champion dinghy sailor and her three-year-old son has inherited the family immunity to seasickness.

They spent most of the last 10 days in the Frisian Islands, exploring the setting of Erskine Childers' classic novel, *The Riddle of the Sands*. Now they needed to make a fast passage home to Harwich if they were to be back at work on time.

The northerly wind on their starboard quarter suited them well. It had risen steadily for the last four hours and, as night fell, they tucked a third slab in the main, rolled away the genoa and set the heavy weather jib on the inner forestay. Speed dropped from an average of nine knots to seven but steering was easier. There were fewer exhilarating surfs on the quartering sea but she seemed generally under better control.

At 2345 Mary went below to wake the boys for their watch. She was just reaching out of the companionway to hook on when Howard shouted the warning. He heard, rather than saw, the approaching wave. It seemed about twice the size of anything they had experienced that evening and as it broke, it sounded more like an express train than a wave. They were smothered by its breaking crest, slewed to starboard and rolled so fast that Howard was convinced that they would roll right over. But they didn't, they paused upside down before slowly righting.

Howard spun the wheel to port to bear away but she would not respond and lay with the wind and sea just forward of the starboard beam. It didn't take him long to realise that either the steering was smashed or the rudder had gone.

Mary struggled back into the cockpit, closely followed by the rest of the crew. The water that had poured down the open hatch was, they reported, close to bunk level. They thought that the forehatch had been smashed. Their account of the chaos below was interrupted by a second breaking wave. Again the boat heeled violently but this time righted herself from about 90 degrees. Everyone managed to hang on but a lot more water had gone down below. Howard glanced at his daughter, his three-year-old grandson in her arms. 'How long can they hang on in this?', he asked himself.

Howard took stock of the situation. The boat was lying beam on to the sea, the wind had risen well above gale force. He cursed himself for his failure to notice how bad conditions were getting before the first roll. His mind turned to the liferaft. It had a hydrostatic release but, should they sink suddenly, it would almost certainly snag in the rigging as the boat went down. He had no time to hesitate. The lives of his family were much more important than his precious boat. He shouted, 'Abandon ship!' and moved forward to release the liferaft from its cradle.

Has he made the right decision?

What would you do?

Probably not, but it's easy to see why he has decided to abandon ship so soon. His disabled boat has been knocked flat twice in as many minutes, there's a wild sea running, seven people in the cockpit, one of them a toddler and probably only two wearing harnesses or lifejackets.

He needs to get his crew into foul weather gear, safety harnesses and lifejackets. Next he needs to make a better assessment of the amount of water in the boat, send a distress call then assess and – if necessary and if possible – repair the damage to watertight integrity and start pumping. He doesn't have to do all this himself though, he has plenty of strength and experience in the crew to delegate.

He may quickly decide that the boat really is sinking, in which case he will have to abandon. He may, on the other hand, find that the forehatch is simply open or easy enough to plug and, once the companionway hatch is closed, it too is watertight. A relatively small amount of water can at first seem alarming in a boat that is crashing about in a seaway.

His initial reaction is that he is in grave and imminent danger and needs immediate assistance, so he should certainly send the distress call. The batteries maybe about to submerge and he could be left without power. He can always downgrade the Mayday to urgency, or cancel it, if he finds that he is able to maintain watertight integrity, restore some measure of directional control and pump the boat dry.

It is not an easy decision but history suggests that if there is any chance of saving the boat, she will offer a better chance of survival than taking to the liferaft.

EXTRA HELP NEEDED?

06

Q David had decided years ago that the cruising ground he'd known all his life was no longer a sensible place to base a yacht. It was crowded at weekends and he had cruised everywhere within range. His family were reluctant to accompany him in weather that they deemed too cold and wet for sailing. He now owned a quarter share in a Mediterranean-based cruiser that his family loved and David got his evening and weekend sailing in a Wayfarer dinghy in Chichester.

On the evening in question he was sailing in the harbour's almost deserted waters with his 12-year-old grandson Paul. The only other boat under way was a Finn single-handed dinghy. The wind was gusty and he was concentrating on sailing his own boat rather than watching the single-hander so he didn't notice the accident until Paul burst into laughter and pointing at the other boat, 'that silly man, he forgot to put his feet under the toe straps before he leant out so he nearly did a backward somersault before he hit the water'.

Luckily the hapless single-hander had managed to hang onto his mainsheet and had kept contact with his boat as it capsized. He was a large man and as he climbed onto the centreboard his boat quickly righted. David expected to see him climb aboard and sail on. But he didn't. The capsize had been brief, the boat had floated high on its side and righted without shipping any water. The helmsman's bulk, which had been an asset in righting his boat, was now a distinct hindrance. He had dropped into the water as he righted the boat and now, hampered by a rather bulky buoyancy aid, he couldn't climb back on board.

David tacked round and sailed back towards the struggling single-hander. He had tried without success to climb over the windward side. He moved to the stern to see if he could haul himself over the transom but no luck there either. He was clearly tiring. David hailed him. 'Do you want a hand?'. The reply was immediate; 'Yes please. I can't haul myself over the windward side or the stern and if I try to climb in from leeward she'll capsize on top of me.' The helmsman was now on the windward side of his boat, which was lying beam to the wind with its single sail shaking.

David wondered how to approach the Finn so that he could help. If he tried to come alongside to windward his own mainsail might prevent him getting close enough to grab the dinghy and there was also a risk of crushing the sailor hanging onto her. A leeward approach would be hampered by the other boat's mainsail. If he tried to come head to wind across her bow there would be a chance he would loose steerage way, pay off alongside her and the rigs would tangle. He didn't have a handheld VHF but did have a mobile phone in a waterproof bag with which he could ask the coastguard to get help.

What would you do?

A David's first move should be to ask the single-hander if he can make a loop, probably the end of the main halyard, the right length to put his foot in and climb back onboard. If he can't then David should ask him to let go of his boat and swim clear so that he can be picked from the water without risk of tangling the dinghies' rigs or crushing anyone between the two hulls. It might seem wrong to ask the casualty to disobey the basic rule of staying with the boat but he is in a buoyancy aid, help is close at hand and there is less risk in picking him out of the water than trying to rescue him from alongside his boat.

When he lets go of his boat it may well capsize again and once he is out of the water he'll still need to get on board his boat again. With any luck he will decide that he has had enough swimming and be happy to take a lift home with you, making arrangements with his sailing club, a friend or the harbourmaster to collect his dinghy with a motor boat. If he wants to try to get back on board, David could lower his mainsail and make the approach under jib, which would greatly reduce the risk of damage or tangling rigs.

WHICH PORT IN A STORM?

07

Q Northeasterly gales are not particularly common in the English Channel. Davey couldn't actually remember when he had last encountered one but the forecast was unambiguous. A vigorous little low would move up-channel during the day, the wind would increase and back southerly, before continuing to back into the northeast and increasing to Force 8, locally 9 overnight.

When he and his family had berthed in the little visitors' yacht haven the previous evening in a moderate westerly, he had congratulated himself on finding an outside northeast facing berth, no squeaky fenders and a good night's sleep for all. He wondered whether he dared stay in it.

The yacht haven was well protected from the south and west but it was open to a three-mile fetch from the northeast. That would mean a nasty little chop, fenders popping out and the chance of cosmetic, or even structural damage to topsides. His 26-footer was a tough boat but by modern standards she was small. He could probably get away with staying where he was as long as a larger boat didn't arrive alongside, putting a great deal of extra weight on his fenders and, should they fail, on the boat herself.

He considered the alternatives. The wind was already a blustery southerly and the bright sunshine of the early morning had faded to a threatening grey overcast sky. All the well-sheltered inner berths in the yacht haven were rafted two or three deep and he did not like the idea of trying to squeeze into any of the remaining tight spaces in the freshening wind. Delicate berthing manoeuvres were never simple with two young children in the crew; looking after them reduced their effective adult manpower to little less than a single-hander.

There were no sheltered berths alongside or mooring buoys within easy sailing distance. The only other option was an anchor berth in the upper reaches of the river. The holding ground there was good and the shelter of the high wooded banks should be excellent. The snag was that in a gale it would be dangerous to use the dinghy.

His train of thought was interrupted by his younger son. 'Daddy, you said that the next time we were stuck in harbour with foul weather we could go to the cinema so can we go, please?'. Support for the suggestion was immediately forthcoming from his older brother. So does Davey head up river and risk a mutiny, or stay put for family harmony and put up with the overnight mayhem of a bouncy marina?

The last gust was a lot stronger than the one before and the rain has just started so he has to make a quick decision.

What would you do?

The trouble with a crowded marina in a gale is that you are dependent on other people's seamanship and common sense for your safety. When you are in one of the smaller boats in the area that is an unpleasant prospect. In fact very few boats in marinas suffer more than cosmetic damage in summer gales and if a real storm develops you do have the option of abandoning ship with feet more or less dry.

A well-sheltered anchor berth, particularly if it is not overcrowded, offers a more tranquil option, provided that you can avoid the situation where the wind funnels along the reach in which you are anchored. A strong wind against tide will cause the boat to veer around wildly and snatch at her anchor from different directions. As long as you can find a cross-wind reach – the harder it blows the better – a well set anchor will dig in. You just need to watch out on the turn of the tide when the direction of pull may cause it to break out. Davey should head for the anchorage. It would offer a better chance of a reasonable night's sleep with much less likelihood of damage to the boat. The challenge of keeping a young crew entertained until the gale blows over seems a fair price to pay.

WHICH WAY TO TURN?

08

Q It had been a nerve-racking couple of hours crossing the shipping lanes, sailing close hauled on port tack in a gusty Force 5 with visibility anything from two to 10 miles in rain showers. At last they seemed to be clear of ships, the only light visible was the single green of the other yacht which had been following them all night, broad on the port quarter, probably no more than a couple of hundred yards away.

Jane and Peter had been on watch for half an hour and were well settled in so Nick decided that he could safely go below for a couple of hour's sleep. He paused in the companionway for a last look round and noticed to his dismay another single green light, fine on the port bow. He pointed it out to Peter, who took a bearing. Nick kept it lined up with the forward stanchion on the port side and it was no surprise when, two minutes later, Peter reported that the bearing seemed steady.

Peter summed up the situation. 'I reckon he's about a mile away and running more or less square. Goodness knows which tack he's on but one of us is going to have to alter course. If he's on port then as windward boat he's got to move. If he's on starboard then we have to alter and our options are a bit limited by our friend so close on the port quarter. I wonder if he's seen the newcomer? He's probably just working out whether or not he's got to give way to her too.'

Nick knew that he didn't have long to make a decision. The boat to windward probably had a relative speed of closing of about 12 knots, which meant that he was just some five minutes away from a collision. His train of thought was interrupted by Jane at the helm, who had obviously been working out the situation herself.

'Tack now, skipper?', she asked.

Again Nick hesitated. If he tacked he would have right of way over the other close-hauled boat but if she was only 200 yards away then he would be relying on her lookout to be really alert and her helmsman to be ready to throw a quick tack to avoid him. And what if the boat to windward were coming down really fast under spinnaker? If he got this one wrong there would be chaos. He glanced at the two green lights, the bearings of both seemed to be rock steady. His inclination was to go with Jane's suggestion and tack but that would put him straight across the bows of the nearest boat. If only it was daylight he would be able to see which tack the boat running towards them was on.

Enough thinking, it's time for action.

What would you do?

A Sailing at night, do you always have the main and genoa sheets ready to run free? If so you can go for the only really safe manoeuvre and gybe round the stern of the boat on your port quarter.

The really difficult thing about this situation is that you can't be sure what the other two boats are about to do so there is the danger of a series of self-cancelling manoeuvres. Night-time collision avoidance manoeuvres are best when they result in the other people involved seeing a different colour of light. If you gybe to pass astern of the boat on your port quarter she will see your light change from white to green and start to draw rapidly right so she will know that she is clear to tack – probably her preferred option for avoiding the boat to windward – or to bear way. The boat to windward will see your red light change to white and then to green as you harden up having cleared the stern of your neighbour so he knows that you are no longer a problem.

If you don't keep the sheets well sorted in the cockpit you may have a problem gybing at short notice so you'll have to work out your own solution – and the best of luck with it.

A LOVELY DAY OUT?

09

Dick cursed under his breath. It had seemed like a really good idea when he had volunteered his boat, on a beautiful spring morning, for the office day out. And it would have been a good idea if the appointed date in July had been just as warm and sunny. But it wasn't, the previous evening's forecast had been for strong winds and blustery showers and now, driving down to Chichester Harbour, the first showers had arrived and they were certainly blustery.

He had thought about ringing round and postponing the outing but that wouldn't have been easy. Seven telephone calls, some of them no doubt to answering machines and then the difficulty of finding another day before the end of the summer when all eight of them were free. It wasn't as if it was going to blow a gale, with an experienced crew it would be a great day's sailing, he was just going to have to take things gently.

One of the difficulties he would have to cope with would be the crowd in the cockpit. It was roomy for a 36-footer but the mainsheet track running across the forward end of it was a potential hazard for the non-sailors. The only other person onboard with any real sailing experience would be young Peter who was a keen dinghy sailor. Three of the others were fit and enthusiastic sports players but that left three who would be real passengers. As usual when he was about to go for a sail with non-sailing friends he wished that he didn't have a boat with running backstays.

The local forecast on the notice board at the Marina Office promised a Southwest Force 5, gusting 6, locally 7 round exposed headlands. Dick walked down to the boat and climbed on board, wondering what sort of day out he was going to be able to lay on. His original plan had been an eight mile sail across to Seaview on the Isle of Wight, anchor for lunch and sail back for dinner in the marina. The four more adventurous members of the group should have a great day and the other three would love boasting about the 'storm' they had survived.

The alternatives were a sail, or a motor, round the harbour, anchor off East Head for lunch and a walk over the sand dunes. That would certainly be a safer option, nobody would be seasick and as long as they managed to do some sailing it would be adventurous enough to meet his boss's suggestion that a day with a bit of spice to it would be good for team building.

His ponderings were interrupted by Peter's cheerful greeting. 'Lovely day for a sail. Do you want me to tuck a couple of reefs in the main and get a headsail ready before the others arrive?'

It is decision time for Dick. The choices are: the full adventure to Seaview, the safe and cautious option of a rather tame motor round Chichester Harbour or the half way house of staying in the harbour but getting some sail up. And if you are going to sail, how many reefs in the main and which headsail do you want? The headsail options are a rolling genoa or a storm jib on an inner forestay.

What would you do?

Eight miles to windward on a blustery showery day seems rather a long way for non-sailors. Dick and Peter would enjoy it, as might the more adventurous colleagues but the three more sedentary members of the team would very likely have a miserable time.

Motoring round the harbour and a walk would certainly be the safe option but rather a waste of a day in a sailing boat. The compromise of a sail in the harbour seems attractive but sailing in confined waters with too many people and not enough experience on board needs care. There has been an alarming number of head injuries on corporate hospitality days out in boats with mainsheet travellers in overcrowded cockpits. But they came for a sail and with care they can have one.

I would opt for the roller genoa and leave the main stowed. Most modern boats sail surprisingly well under headsail alone and with no main set you can leave both runners made up and allow your passengers to steer, which they will love, without having to worry about maiming anyone in an accidental gybe. And if things do start to get alarming in one of the promised gusts you can reduce or even get rid of the sail on any point of sailing and resort to motor. With any luck you won't have to and everyone can go home at the end of the day with a great story of how they steered your boat through a gale!

LEADING FROM BEHIND?

Q James and Richard desperately wanted to get their Yachtmaster tickets so that they could get jobs as crew during their gap year between school and university. They were both good dinghy sailors, they had done the shore-based course the previous winter, the practical course in the spring and now all they needed was to gain qualifying seatime before taking the exam. Since neither of them owned, or had access to, a cruising boat the quickest and least expensive way to log the necessary sea miles and passages seemed to be to sign on as volunteer crew with a yacht delivery company.

Four hours into their first offshore passage, returning a 36-footer from Treguier, where her owner had left her storm bound at the end of his summer holiday, to her home port of Falmouth, they began to wonder if it had been such a good idea.

The journey out from home had been tedious. A sleepless overnight ferry from Plymouth to Roscoff, two trains and a taxi ride had brought them to Treguier by lunch. They had grabbed a quick bite to eat in the café by the marina, checked over the boat and caught the first of the ebb down river. Now they were off the North Brittany coast, sailing fast in a brisk southwesterly. The early sunshine had given way to total cloud cover half way down the river and it had just started to rain. The sea was building and both of the youngsters had started to feel queasy.

The 1754 shipping forecast had not been encouraging, with the southwesterly wind forecast to increase 6-8, locally 9 and veer northwesterly, decreasing 5-7 later. Their skipper had not been particularly communicative since they met at the ferry terminal the previous evening and the forecast of a gale on the nose had done little to improve his already sullen mood.

He announced his plan for the night. He would cook supper now and then turn in for four hours, leaving the boys on watch until 0100. Then they could have four

hours in their bunks, so it would be daylight before they would have to be on deck again. He didn't expect the weather to get too lively before the small hours but he had already seen that the boys knew how to shorten sail without leaving the cockpit and they shouldn't hesitate to call him if they had any worries.

On their own in the cockpit, Richard and James pondered their immediate future. A hundred miles to go, dark in an hour and the weather set to get a great deal worse, it was not a happy prospect.

'Not much of a leader, our brave skipper,' muttered James.

'Quite agree,' Richard replied. 'I'd have thought that someone with his experience would have learnt that the best way to lead was by example, take the first night watch himself and let less experienced people like us get some sleep before we have to do battle with a severe gale.'

Are the youngsters right? Should their skipper have made a different plan for the night?

What would you do?

A I don't have any problem with the plan, although I hope I would have done a better job of explaining it to my crew.

A hot meal is important before nightfall and the experienced skipper is more likely to be able to cook it without succumbing to seasickness. The first half of the night, before the wind heads and strengthens, is likely to hold fewer problems than the second. It is important for the skipper, as the most experienced person on board, to snatch a few hours sleep before the going gets really rough, so that he can make the best possible job of setting the boat up to make progress to windward, or snugging her down hove-to when the worst of the weather hits. According to the forecast the strongest winds will be fairly short lived and the skipper's plan is probably as good as possible for dealing with them.

If he just explained it all to his crew he might have a happier ship.

Q George surveyed the berth (see 'A' in the diagram), or what he could see of it through the driving rain.

The wind was strong and gusty, the river was running at about two knots, it was getting dark and his only crew member, his 14-year-old son Richard, was going to struggle to get ashore with the headrope and take a turn round the cleat at the western end of the pontoon before the bows started to blow off the berth. He would just have to make the approach dead head to wind and as fast as he dared so that he stood some chance of holding the bows alongside for a few seconds. As long as Richard could get the headrope secured she would lie to it like a dinghy on her painter and he could take his time about heaving her close alongside.

He passed the helm to Richard, with instructions to use just enough throttle to hold her head to wind while he readied the warps and fenders. With everything on deck ready and double checked he relieved Richard of the helm and was just lining up for the approach when, to his great relief, an oilskinned figure appeared on the pontoon.

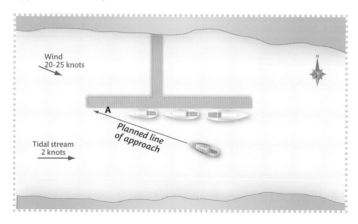

'Don't worry,' he hailed, 'I'll take your lines for you, no problem at all.'

George changed his plan slightly, and his instructions to Richard. 'Don't worry about jumping onto the pontoon, just pass the end of the headrope to our helper. Don't try to throw it against the wind, if he fails to catch it the end will be round our prop in seconds. I'll swing her alongside at the last moment and drop a bight of the back-spring over the cleat on the pontoon.'

The approach was near perfect, he swung the boat parallel to the pontoon, the headrope was passed, the stranger moved towards the cleat at the end of the pontoon and George seemed to have ample time to leave the tiller and drop the bight of his back-spring over the cleat on the pontoon.

He was starting to congratulate himself on a difficult manoeuvre well executed when a stronger gust rattled the rigging. He quickly took down the slack on the back-spring and glanced forward. To his horror he saw that the bow was being blown quickly to port and the helper on the pontoon, rather than taking a turn round the cleat with the headrope, was wrapping it round his hand and struggling to keep his footing as he started to lose the impossible tug of war with six tons of boat.

Put yourself in Georges's place. He has about two seconds to decide what to do and another two seconds to do it.

What would you do?

There are very few occasions when it helps to shout in a boat but I think this is one of them. George needs to bellow 'Richard, cast off the headrope!' Whether or not Richard is able to carry out this instruction rather depends on how well George made the headrope ready in the first place. If he has one round turn and a couple of figures of eight around the cleat, with the end tidy and clear to run, then Richard is in with a chance. If he has put a locking hitch over the final turn or worse still a bowline in the end and dropped the loop over the cleat then all is probably lost, the helper on the pontoon is about to start swimming and George has a huge problem on his hands.

Why Richard rather than the helper as the one to let go the headrope? Partly because the helper, having started to wind the line around his hand, probably won't be able to free it, and partly because if he does, the end will be carried aft towards the prop. Simply shouting 'Let go the headrope!' which could be directed at the person on either end of the line is liable to prompt a 'Who, me?' reaction.

At the same time he is asking for the headrope to be cast off, George needs to slip the back-spring. As soon as he has done so he will take a lot of the weight off the headrope but I doubt if just slipping the back-spring will be enough to relieve the load on the helper sufficiently for him to retain his tenuous foothold on the pontoon.

What George must not do is attempt to relieve the situation by trying to motor ahead, even with the helm hard to starboard to bring the bow back in towards the berth. With the back-spring tight the stern can't swing to port so the bow can't possibly swing to starboard. Any use of the engine is simply going to hasten the helper's plunge.

Q Clive was regretting his spur of the moment offer to his old friend Nick to crew for him on a delivery passage. The two of them needed to make the 320-mile passage from Cork to Lymington, Nick's home port, over a three-day holiday weekend.

All had gone well on the long offshore leg, to Land's End under engine in a flat calm for the first few hours then an increasing southwesterly wind giving fast reaching. As they crossed Mount's Bay the wind had gone much lighter. They were on a very rolly dead run with no more than a Force 3 and a big swell.

Over the change of watch at 2000 Nick suggested that they rig a preventer to steady the main boom and reduce the risk of an accidental gybe during the night. Clive wasn't keen on the idea. They already had the genoa boomed out, with the spinnaker sheet, guy and topping lift holding the boom in place. With the preventer on the main as well there was going to be an awful lot of rope leading back to cleats in the cockpit, a complication which Clive did not want to deal with if he had to alter course for shipping or re-trim the sails for a windshift during the night.

He had painful memories of a number of regrettable incidents with preventers in the past. One involved a gybe on a very windy run that ended up with the boat flat on her side, pinned there by the backed main, held vertical against the preventer. Another had led to a near miss with a coaster when he had to call up the watch below to release the preventer which had snarled round a mooring cleat on the foredeck before he could gybe and turn to starboard. The third was a broken boom, the result of a violent gybe against a preventer rigged from the middle of it.

In his own boat he would have steered with care to reduce the possibility of an accidental gybe. It probably wouldn't have done any damage in such light winds so it would have been a lesser risk than having the over-complication of an additional line, holding the rig rigid and restricting manoeuvrability. Before he could voice his concerns, however, Nick was busy rigging the preventer, from the outer end of the boom, through a block on the foredeck and back to a cleat on the cockpit coaming.

Clive realised giving voice to his misgivings was now going to be difficult. Should he just accept that in another man's boat he had little option but to accept that things would not necessarily be done his way or should he have the courage of his convictions and explain why he would prefer to sail without the preventer?

What would you do?

A Clive seems to me to be worrying unnecessarily. A light wind and a big swell is a combination that is almost bound to lead to an accidental gybe and even though there is little wind the repeated banging of the boom against the main sheet is going to put unnecessarily heavy loads on the rig. There is also the possibility of injury if someone in the cockpit is caught in the falls of the mainsheet as the boom crashes across.

Clive's previous misadventures with preventers happened because he was using a badly rigged preventer or using it in the wrong circumstances.

A badly rigged preventer, or a preventer used when there is no need for it, can certainly be a lot more trouble than it is worth. In this case the only alternatives are to use one or continue the passage on a series of broad reaches rather than a dead run, and in a big swell with a light wind even a broad reach is going to give a lot of chafe in the rig which would be better avoided.

A FAST PASSAGE?

13

Q Leaving Lymington at 0900 after a hearty breakfast, Nick was looking forward to a fast passage west to Weymouth. A fresh southeast wind should give him a broad reach all the way. An average speed of seven knots should be achievable so he should knock off the 40 mile passage in about six hours. He unrolled the main and genoa and bore away anticipating a cracking good sail.

Weymouth Harbour

Weymouth Bay

•**Weymouth**

N

Portland Harbour

Wind SE

Isle of Portland

☼ **Bill of Portland**

0   2nm

And so it was, for the first hour or so, but once out of the lee of the land the sea began to build it became clear that the autopilot was not going to cope. He would be on the helm for the whole passage.

To make the steering easier he rolled away half of the furling main, which took most of the weight off the tiller and cost very little speed. This was going to be a longer spell than Nick was used to, he very seldom sailed the boat single handed but he didn't anticipate any difficulty in coping and the alternative of breaking the passage by putting in to Poole seemed like a waste of a fair breeze.

Five hours later, approaching his destination, Nick congratulated himself on his decision to carry on single handed. It had been a great sail, one he wouldn't have missed for the world.

Half a mile off Weymouth's narrow harbour entrance he started the engine and set about furling the genoa. He heaved on the furling line but encountered solid resistance. He tried easing the sheet, but to no avail. The furling gear still seemed locked. He tried the furling line on the main and encountered no resistance so at least he would have no problem getting rid of the mainsail. He brought the boat round onto a close reach to see if he could shift whatever was jamming the headsail roller. As he came onto the wind he realised that he had much too much sail up, the lee rail dipped, the genoa flogged wildly and the furling gear still refused to budge. Peering forward he could now see why. He had left a short warp on the foredeck that had rolled in with the furling line and formed a solid knot on the drum.

Nick was going to have to lower the genoa or attempt to berth with it still fully set. Lowering it single-handed was not going to be easy, the halyard was led aft to the cockpit so he would have difficulty controlling the rate of lowering and gathering the sail on the foredeck at the same time. The alternative of going into the fairly tight harbour, downwind with the full genoa set and putting the boat alongside on his own was equally unappealing.

Nick cursed himself for not realising earlier how much the wind had freshened, but it was too late now to worry about that.

What would you do?

Taking the boat into Weymouth, single handed, with the full genoa set would certainly be high risk. As he enters the harbour the wind is bound to go flukey with patches of calm and unpredictable gusts. If he motors with the sheets free he risks a sheet round the prop. If he secures a sheet he risks being spun by an unexpected header before he can free. It's a no win situation.

He needs to get rid of the genoa but he needs to make sure that as he lowers it the sail doesn't go over the side. This means he has to be on the foredeck as the sail comes down and to have some way of encouraging the sail to drop onto the deck and not over the side. One way to do this would be to motor slowly head to wind under autopilot, flake out the halyard ready to run, take it off the cleat and head for the foredeck with a bunch of sail ties to secure the genoa to the guard rail as it comes down. It is unlikely to drop too quickly, he is going to have to pull it down. The risk is that he will damage the sail or himself as it flogs over the deck or he will lose control of it, the sail will go in the water and round the prop, turning a problem into a disaster.

Another way to get the sail down would be to heave to before lowering. He will still have to control and secure the sail but with no engine running the consequences of ropes or sails over the side will be less dire. The problem will be to nip back to the cockpit quickly as soon as the sail is lowered to stop the boat tacking and gybing after there is no headsail to keep the boat hove to but if he can get her to heave to with a fairly slack mainsheet this should not be to much of a problem.

He also has the option of sailing into Portland Harbour, anchoring and then lowering the genoa. Again, this could work but in a southeasterly the shelter in the harbour is not good and he risks finishing up with a dragging anchor, a wildly flogging genoa and a lee shore coming up fast.

I would go for heaving to and lowering because it offers the least potential for worsening the situation. If Nick had discovered the problem earlier he would have had sea room to broad reach off under auto pilot (an exact course wouldn't matter much), possibly with the main fully furled while he sorted the snarl up on the headsail reefing drum.

THE NEED FOR SPEED?

14

Q Mary had chosen the date for the family summer holiday with great care, as early as possible in the school holidays. Ideally she would have liked an easterly wind and a fair tide to take them from Hamble down to Poole but that was something she couldn't arrange six months in advance.

They had travelled down to the boat on the Friday evening in continuous rain but the forecast for the Saturday morning promised sunshine and a moderate northwesterly, not ideal but at least not dead on the nose. They left Hamble as planned at 0900 and headed south down Southampton Water. It was a beautiful clear day and Mary soon noticed that there was an unusually large number of boats apparently sailing round in circles. She recoiled at the distant sound of a cannon – she hadn't thought of everything after all. It was Cowes week.

'What fun!', said Pippa, her elder daughter, 'That means there will be plenty to watch instead of the usual boring old sailing.'

Mary wasn't quite so sure, reckoning that within an hour or so their path would be thick with testosterone-fuelled racing boats cursing all innocent cruisers for wandering onto their race track. The children might enjoy it but it was the sort of tension-building sail her husband Peter hated and which generally led to considerable disharmony on board. It came as no surprise when Peter, realising that they were about to stray into the biggest regatta of the year, suggested that it might be a good idea to tuck into Beaulieu and wait for the evening before continuing west.

The moans of dismay that greeted Peter's suggestion made it very clear that this was a decision that he wouldn't be allowed to take without provoking a mutiny. He thought about the next couple of hours. With the northwesterly wind they would be on a close reach or even close hauled on starboard, heading just south of west all the way to Yarmouth, with every other boat having to give way to them. Maybe it would be OK after all, certainly better than upsetting his wife and both daughters within an hour of setting sail.

At first it was, as Pippa had suggested, a really fun sail, with boats dashing past, heavily overcanvassed, crews perched on the weather rail and they didn't seem to be in anyone's way. But off Newtown River things started to get ugly as the number of racing marks increased. They were surrounded by the back end of a cruiser class when one of them tacked off their port bow and came charging towards them.

'Out of the way, Water for a boat racing!' shouted her helmsman.

Peter glanced over his weather quarter, a racer close hauled on starboard overtaking them close to windward. On his leeward quarter another racing boat coming up fast. Mary resolved the situation for him. In a voice much louder than Peter had ever heard her use she yelled at the approaching port tacker 'STARBOARD!'

His shouted response was unprintable but he tacked, narrowly missing another racing boat in the process. Peter was mortified. 'I said we shouldn't have mixed it with this bunch of hooligans, it was bound to get us into trouble.'

A ringside seat for the racing or a happy day exploring the Beaulieu river.

What would you do?

I don't think they got it wrong. Racing boats have no special rights over the rest of the sea-going world but life is more pleasant when both racers and cruisers exercise common sense and good manners.

There are times when it makes sense to keep out of the way of a racing fleet. It would be pretty stupid to barge through the starting line on which 100 dinghies are massed, waiting for the off and they would be a compact little bunch, requiring only a minor diversion to leave them to their highly competitive brand of fun. Similarly the start of a high profile ocean race, which attracts thousands of spectators, demands special local rules with prohibited areas to give the competitors a fair chance of a decent start.

A larger regatta, with multiple classes, racing in the Western Solent is a rather different matter. If you have to sail through their racing area you will need to have your wits about you and to avoid the areas of highest congestion, such as turning marks and starting lines. However most racing yachts happily accept that cruising boats have every right to the same patch of sea as them and as long as both racers and cruisers behave reasonably predictably the potential conflicts are easy enough to avoid.

The front end of any fleet is unlikely to give trouble, the boats are competently sailed and they won't waste time picking fights with cruisers. Mr Shouty who tried to make life difficult for Peter and Mary is, unfortunately, a feature of most racing fleets. He is to be found close to the back end, where he blames everyone but himself for his miserable performance. Be ready to get out of his way because he may be so incompetent that he can't get out of yours but as a general rule Mary's treatment of him works well. Nobody should have the slightest regret about firmly insisting that he sticks to the rules, his fellow competitors will be delighted to see him put in his place so Peter can relax and enjoy the sail with a totally clear conscience.

CORNERED?

Q Ever since they started sailing together John and Mary had shared the skipper and crew roles, taking it in turns to be the one in charge. Today, John was the crew. When they arrived at the marina the previous evening there had been just one berth vacant. The initial approach to it had not been particularly easy, but once more or less in position off the berth and parallel to it, the westerly breeze had taken care of the final stage of the manoeuvre.

The forecast had been for the wind to veer 180° during the night so they had anticipated an equally simple departure. However, by 0600, the chosen hour for leaving, the wind was still a fraction south of west. They could not delay departure for long and so had to set off within the next half hour.

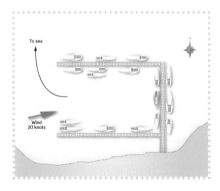

Their boat had superb sea-keeping ability but as is often the case it was at the expense of a certain lack of handiness for manoeuvring in tight harbours. She was traditional in shape, with a long keel, high bow, and transom stern. There was very little sideways kick from the prop, ahead or astern, but her turning circle was large. She was quick to gain steerageway when the engine was in ahead but going astern she needed to be making about three knots before the rudder had much control.

John weighed up the situation and decided what he would have done, had it been up to him. He would have rigged the back spring as a slip, put plenty of fenders on the port quarter and sprung the bow out by motoring astern against the spring. As soon as she was almost head to wind he would have gone ahead firmly, to gain steerageway quickly, and motored off under good control. So it came as a surprise when Margaret asked him to make ready a head spring as a slip, with fenders on the port bow so that she could spring the stern well clear before motoring out astern.

An unwritten rule of John and Margaret's boat management was that the crew should only question the skipper's plan if he thought it was dangerous and might cause damage to a vessel or injury to a person. It was an option that they both used very sparingly so John took a while to consider Margaret's plan.

Put yourself in John's position. Do you really have a safer plan, or just a different one?

What would you do?

A I think that Margaret's plan is the better of the two. John's preferred tactic will only work if he can spring the bow right out to head to wind, which I very much doubt will be possible – there is a limit to how far one can spring out the bow of a boat against the wind.

Even though he will quite quickly have control when he puts the engine ahead it will not be instantaneous. If he takes the risk of going ahead with the wind still on his starboard bow, he will be in danger of the bows being blown off to port before he has enough control to overcome the windage on a high bow, and he will finish up in the southeast corner of the alleyway that he is attempting to leave.

Margaret, on the other hand, has a better chance of being able to force the stern well out from the berth, because as well as motoring against the head spring she can use the prop wash against the rudder to pivot the boat. It will be important to get the boat almost at right angles to the berth so that she doesn't risk scraping the bow along the berth as she gathers way astern.

When she goes astern she will initially have little control with the rudder but the high bow means the boat's natural tendency will be to go stern-to the wind – exactly where she wants it to go. It will be vital to make sure that she has adequate fendering on the port bow and to check that there is no cleat or other obstruction on the pontoon on which she could damage the flare of the bow.

Is there a better plan? A tow off the berth from a marina workboat would be a possibility, but it's still very early and anyway it should not really be necessary in 20 knots of onshore wind. Springing the boat out of the berth stern first will involve quite firm use of engine and warps, but as long as the fendering is good, it should be quite a straightforward manoeuvre.

Q Claire was beginning to relax. It had been a harrowing passage from the Hamble to Newhaven, with visibility deteriorating and a westerly wind building all the way. Now, with the GPS showing just three miles to go to the penultimate waypoint, half a mile south of the breakwater light, she could anticipate the relief of sailing into smooth water with an hour of daylight left.

Claire had been on the tiller since rounding the Owers cardinal mark, five hours ago. Her husband, Dan, who had planned the passage, retired to his bunk with a bucket to hand. Claire glanced at the GPS repeater, just over a mile to go to the waypoint. She peered into the murk on the port bow, now slightly anxious that she could see no sign of the breakwater or the land beyond. She had estimated the visibility at just over a mile. With half a mile to go she was becoming seriously anxious.

At the waypoint she turned to port, the GPS now indicating a northerly course and half a mile to go to the harbour entrance. The echosounder showed 14 m, more or less what she expected.

With a quarter of a mile to go according to the GPS and still no sight of the breakwater her nerve failed. Remembering what her father had taught her about never closing the coast when unsure of her position, she tacked the boat, heading away from the land towards deep water and hove-to.

Dan was now wide awake and, by the sound of things, making good use of his bucket. Claire lashed the tiller to leeward and went below to get a fix on the chart. The problem that had caused the missed landfall soon became apparent. The final two waypoints had been wrongly entered in the GPS with a longitude of 0°3.9′W, instead of East.

Two hours later, snugly secured in Newhaven, Claire decided that there was little point in recriminations. Dan had fouled up on the passage planning and by his hangdog expression he was painfully well aware of the fact.

'My fault,' said Claire. 'I should never have sailed for more than an hour without putting a fix on the chart.'

'Shouldn't have needed to,' replied Dan. 'I thought I had double checked all the waypoints, I can't

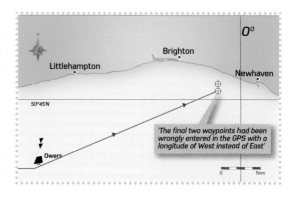

'The final two waypoints had been wrongly entered in the GPS with a longitude of West instead of East'

think how I missed the West for East longitude mistake on two waypoints.'

How can Dan and Claire make sure that they minimise the risk of making the same mistake again?

What would you do?

A Double checking waypoints is a pretty tedious process so any mistake in the original is quite likely to be repeated during the check. One simple way to avoid gross errors is to measure the course and distance for each leg on the chart and compare the chartwork with the courses and distances given by the GPS while the route is compiled. If Dan had followed this process he would certainly have seen the discrepancy between the charted and GPS versions of the distance for the leg from the Owers to Newhaven.

Another routine that helps to avoid repeated errors is to get someone who wasn't involved in compiling the route to check it. A fresh mind is less likely to repeat any errors in the original.

Regular position fixes are very important, but it is easier said than done when sailing shorthanded if the effective crew is severely depleted by seasickness.

GOOD HOLDING?

Q It had been a perfect family holiday, three days spent in a huge natural harbour. The children had explored the creeks and islets in the dinghy, gone swimming, and taken long walks around the nature reserve. But now it seemed that the weather was about to break. The midday forecast had promised wind increasing and backing from west to southwest, with rain by late evening. But by the following morning the wind should have gone round to the northwest and the rain cleared.

Dick had suggested that it might be a good idea to seek the shelter of one of the harbour's marinas or even head west up river for better shelter but the children were reluctant to move. The wind wasn't forecast to be any more than Force 6 and it was all from a westerly direction so they would have good shelter. He talked over the options with his wife and they agreed that it was already too late to head up river and the marina berths would be crowded with other shelter seekers so they might as well stay put.

By the time of the early evening forecast Dick was beginning to regret his decision. The strong wind warning was now a gale warning, it was already blowing quite hard and it had started raining. He consoled himself with the thought that the anchor should be well dug in after three days, veered 10 metres of warp in addition to the 20 metres of chain that was already out and laid out the kedge and warp on the foredeck just in case it should be needed during the night.

They all turned in early but Dick found it hard to sleep. The wind was kicking up a steep and increasingly uncomfortable chop and shortly after midnight the boat's motion seemed to change. He climbed out of his bunk and switched on the echo sounder. It showed 5 metres. He pulled on his foul weather gear and went on deck. It was now pitch dark and they were lying head to wind.

He went forward and saw that the cable was leading dead ahead at long stay. He was reassured that the worst of the conditions were over when suddenly the bows paid off to starboard. He put his foot on the warp and his heart sank as he felt the tell tale vibration of a dragging anchor. He looked at the anchor lights of his two nearest neighbours, they were moving to windward against the background of the distant shore lights in the town.

Dick knew that quick action was needed. The wind was offshore but he had only a couple of hundred yards between the anchor berth and the shore to leeward. If he grounded now he could be aground for days, possibly breaking his rudder too. He had another 20 metres of warp on the bower anchor that he could veer and the kedge, a rather light Bruce with 5 metres of chain and 15 metres of warp ready for immediate use. The engine was ready to start and it had never failed him. But it was pitch dark and the only remotely useful reference marks were the riding lights of the half dozen other boats in the anchorage.

What would you do?

The anchor has broken out. Why it has done so is impossible to tell, it may simply have capsized as the direction of pull changed and be about to re-set itself or it may have collected a ball of clay or weed which will stop it from digging in again.

Dick has to assume the worst, that the anchor is not going to re-set. Veering more cable is unlikely to help and a light kedge is unlikely to hold in a gale of wind. While there is a temptation to try it to buy a little time by veering cable and using the kedge that would probably be a mistake. Weighing two anchors in the dark on a pitching foredeck will be a great deal more difficult than weighing one.

His best chance of success is to get the engine started, hold the boat head to wind while he gets his crew on deck, and then weigh and relay his bower anchor. It will be far from easy in the dark with no navigational lights but it is his only real chance of success. He can use his neighbours' riding lights as a guide, try to work up to the windward side of the channel and use the echo sounder to keep him from over shooting and grounding before he anchors.

It had been a hard night. They had sailed after an early supper to head 30 miles north across the busy shipping lanes before dark, then west through a maze of sandbanks to their home port. Sally hadn't expected to get any rest until they were north of the shipping lanes but she hadn't bargained on having to sail virtually single-handed for the entire night.

The problem had started when her partner, Dick, had retired to his bunk shortly after sailing, complaining of an upset stomach. This wasn't like him, he was generally completely immune to seasickness so Sally reckoned that the seafood at lunch was probably not quite as fresh as it could have been. In any event, he was out of it for the duration of the trip, suffering horribly to judge by the sound effects which emerged from the heads every half hour or so.

Mike, their crew for the weekend, had been sailing with them on round the buoys races for the last two years and he had been fine on the helm during the breezy outward crossing on Friday. It wasn't until darkness fell that Sally discovered that this was his first night sail and he was totally incapable of steering a compass course in the dark. That left her stuck on the helm from 2100 until shortly before 0200, when the light on their waypoint mark, quick flashing three every five seconds, appeared virtually dead on the bow, some 5 miles away.

Sally saw the chance of an hour's rest. It didn't take long to discover that given a reference point outside the boat Mike was quite happy on the helm and could steer a good course. She checked that they couldn't get into trouble by following a curve of pursuit towards the buoy, briefed Mike on the need to keep a good all round lookout, asked him to wake her if he had any doubts about an approaching vessel and in any event before they reached the buoy. She watched Mike for five minutes to see how he was getting on and as soon as she was happy that he was coping well she settled into the forward leeward corner of the cockpit in the expectation of half an hour's much needed sleep.

Normally she had an unusual talent for grabbing sleep under almost any conditions but tonight, tired as she was, she remained wakeful. Something nagged at her mind, keeping sleep away. Why couldn't she rest, she wondered. They were clear of shipping, the visibility was near perfect, the breeze was steady and in spite of his lack of night sailing experience Mike was doing well. Had she forgotten to pass on some vital piece of information?

Is this women's intuition or just an irrational fear of leaving her boat in the hands of a relative unknown?

What would you do?

Sally is quite right not to drift off to sleep and leave Mike on the helm under these conditions. Her problem is one that I first became aware of many years ago when I met a friend who was inspecting the badly damaged bow of his boat. He had sailed a similar course to Sally's the previous night and in the early hours of the morning he had gone below to listen to the forecast and check on his passage plan, leaving an inexperienced helmsman on deck with instructions to steer for the light on the buoy ahead. He had spent longer at the chart table than he expected and was unaware of a problem until there was an almighty thump from up forward. His helmsman had followed his instructions to the letter, steering for the buoy with deadly accuracy – until he hit it.

The helmsman was neither stupid nor malicious, he simply had no experience of judging distance off lights in the dark and the collision came as just as much a surprise to him as it did to his skipper.

'Steer towards the light ahead' may seem like a reasonable instruction to a helmsman but if he is new to night sailing it needs to be modified by some unambiguous advice on how to make sure that he stops heading for the target before he hits it, or better still the skipper needs to be sure to be back in the cockpit before the boat can possibly have reached the buoy.

Q Joyce and Michael had been sailing together for over 30 years, the first 10 with their children as crew and the last 20 as a couple. They'd never really discussed who was responsible for what on the boat, they had each just assumed responsibility for the tasks that seemed best suited to their skills. Michael, as the larger and heavier, took on most of the physical tasks, while Joyce had a natural bent for anything to do with numbers, so looked after the navigation, weather forecasts and anything to do with the VHF. Steering and domestic chores were shared more or less evenly.

Their trip south to Northern Spain was their longest passage, and they had been apprehensive about setting out from the Camaret for the Biscay crossing to La Coruña. The first day and a half saw a moderate northerly breeze with easy sailing and they had been making good progress under full main and boomed-out genoa. There had been little sign of any other boats.

Early in the evening of their second day at sea the wind started to back and freshen – nothing dangerous, but to hold their course they needed to take the spinnaker boom off the genoa and gybe it across onto the same side as the main. They had been enjoying the late afternoon sunshine in the cockpit, the autopilot coping well with the steering, when Michael clipped his harness line to the jackstay and went forward to see to the spinnaker pole.

It should have been a simple enough job with the weather sheet rigged as usual, free to run through the pole-end fitting, but to reduce chafe they had clipped the pole to the stainless O-ring in the clew of the genoa. Michael decided that the simplest way to unrig the pole would be to slacken the topping lift, unclip the inboard end of the pole from the mast, run it inboard and unclip the outboard end from the clew of the sail.

He pulled the release lanyard to free the pole from the mast and pushed to clear it from the ring. It needed all his weight to shift it, but just as he did, a harder gust of wind struck. He lost his grip on the pole and it fired like a huge arrow, straight into his shoulder. He yelled in agony, tottered backwards, tripped over the guardrail and did a backwards half somersault into the sea, cracking his head on the topsides.

It took Joyce less than 30 seconds to disconnect the autopilot, heave the boat to and assess the situation. Michael was floating alongside attached by his harness line, his right shoulder broken or dislocated and blood oozing from the top of his head.

Put yourself in Joyce's position: you are over 100 miles from land, no other vessel in sight and your partner, who is almost twice your weight, is in the water, semi-conscious and unable to help himself.

What would you do?

AWhy are you reading this answer? It's simple enough, either you do or you don't have a plan. And if you are reading this to find out if your plan is a good one, then it isn't. To be any good it must be one that you have worked out and tested. If the test was realistic and the plan worked, well done. If you haven't or it didn't and you sail a lightly crewed boat then it would be a good idea to make a plan and try it out.

The most effective system I have come across consisted of a four to one kicking strap with snap shackles on both ends and a very long rope tail. To use it, the kicking strap was removed from mast and boom and the hauling end was attached to the spinnaker halyard. The halyard was then hoisted so that the upper block was high enough to lift a casualty over the guardrail, with the lower block attached to the end of the casualty's harness line. The tail was taken through a genoa lead block and back to a primary (self tailing) winch. The 8-stone wife in the team who owned the boat had no trouble hoisting her 14-stone husband out of the water using this method.

There are plenty of patent hoisting and parbuckle devices on the market, which are easy enough to use but all are likely to be less effective because they are seldom used. The only figure I know of, which came from a straw poll of some 100 Yachtmaster Instructors, was that skippers experience an actual MOB incident about once every 48 years. Given the lack of use to which any recovery device is likely to be subject and the rate at which boats accumulate gear it would be hard to guarantee that the patent recovery device is immediately available when it is needed. The kicking strap, however, is unlikely to be hidden in a locker when a boat is at sea.

Q It had been a bad morning. John had switched on the GPS to check the route for the passage home, the lettering on the display turned from black to deep purple and then became unreadable. He tried switching it off and on, checked the battery levels and the connections, but all to no avail. For the first time in years he was going to have to put to sea without the reassurance of always having an immediate indication of the direction and distance to the next waypoint.

He consoled himself that he had made the 30-mile passage countless times in the past, he had even been doing it for long enough to have made the journey more often without GPS than with it. The only worry was the threat of fog later in the day but there was nothing amiss with the radar so he should be able to cope with that.

John and his two sons, Peter and Michael, had been sailing in a light northerly breeze that had freshened steadily until, around 1600, when they found themselves bowling along on a broad reach at seven knots. That was when, with very little warning, it started to drizzle. By 1615 visibility was down to under a quarter of a mile.

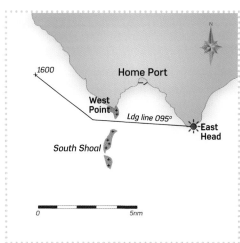

Peter didn't have to be asked to switch on the radar. This was the part of sailing he really enjoyed. He was soon reporting on the few contacts around them and suggesting that there would be no problem picking up the bearing of East Head to put the boat on the leading line through the gap between the rocks off West Point and South Shoal.

At the tiller, John thought about the advisability of going through the half-mile-wide gap on radar. The charted edge of the land should be clear on the radar and most of the coast was low cliffs, which gave a good radar echo. They would get scant help from the echosounder because there was little change in depth until you were right up to the shoals. The northern edge of the channel was exactly half a mile south of West Point so there was little chance of catching a glimpse of it. Peter had never done a radar course but he seemed to have a natural affinity for anything electronic so John felt that he could trust him to do a good job. The set itself was a simple one with few gadgets and gizmos to confuse things and it gave an unstabilised ship's head up picture.

The alternative of going south of the shoals would only add about eight miles to the passage but four of those would be dead to windward. The wind speed was already reading 20 knots relative and it was still increasing. The beat back from the south end of the shoal would be hard going and Peter's younger brother was already starting to turn pale.

Can John trust his son with the navigation and use the short cut between the shoals?

What would you do?

A It should be possible to navigate the channel safely by radar but not by using Peter's preferred method of running the leading bearing on East Head.

Radar bearings are not accurate, particularly when using an unstabilised ship's head-up display. In order to take a bearing Peter needs to know the boat's heading, and as she will probably be yawing at least five degrees either side of course this will be the minimum error he can expect. There will also be some distortion caused by the horizontal beam width of the set, which tends to extend land echos. Any small misalignment between radar and actual ship's heading may account for another couple of degrees of error.

In order to pass safely through the gap the bearing of the leading mark, four miles away, needs to be within four degrees of correct and this is simply outside the tolerance to which even the most experienced navigator could hope to take radar bearings. It wouldn't be that easy using visual bearings on a rough day.

Radar ranges are much more accurate so a method that uses ranges rather than bearings would be much better. My preferred method would be to close the coast just north of West Point to a distance of $^7/_{10}$ of a nautical mile, then steer to maintain that distance off the land until clear southeast of the point. That way you should pass through the middle of the safe water.

A purist might suggest running a parallel index of $^7/_{10}$ of a nautical mile off the point on a heading of 095° but with the unstabilised radar that would be much harder than simply keeping the distance off the coast.

Q Margaret braced her feet against the lee side bench to get better purchase on the tiller. The wind had certainly strengthened in the last half hour and it was becoming more difficult to stop the boat from griping in the gusts. She glanced at the log, it was showing over six knots, not bad for a 27-footer on a beam reach with a reef in the main and four rolls in the headsail, but if the wind went on building they would soon need to shorten sail again.

Dick appeared in the companionway, smiling wryly. 'Not a great forecast,' he said. 'Westerly, 4–5 locally 6, but increasing 7, locally 8 later. By the look of the sea we're getting the locally 6 now but I suppose that's to be expected round the south of the Isle of Wight where it gets squeezed past St Catherine's Point.'

They had known when they left Cherbourg in a light westerly the previous evening, bound for Chichester, that the wind was likely to strengthen during the passage but there had been no mention of gales or anything stronger than Force 6. The other two crew members, their nine year-old twin boys, had slept soundly all the way, securely tucked into the quarter berths and helped no doubt by a liberal dose of seasickness remedy.

Margaret did a little mental navigation. With 25 miles still to go to Chichester entrance they should, at the present speed, be there in four hours. With any luck the boys would sleep until at least 0800 so they would only be awake for the last couple of hours of the trip and by that time they should be starting to feel some shelter from the Isle of Wight.

Another gust stuck, again making it difficult to hold her on course.

'Time to shorten sail again,' said Dick. 'With that forecast I think we should go straight to the storm jib and fully reefed main now, we don't want to be struggling to shorten sail in a full gale.'

'Do we really need to do anything quite so drastic?' asked Margaret. 'She's not too hard to steer yet. I think we need all the speed we can squeeze out of her, particularly with that forecast.'

SLOW DOWN OR SPEED UP?

Dick was tempted by his partner's 'go for it' approach, yet he was hesitant about agreeing with it. They had, after all, never set the storm jib in anger and neither had they ever needed to use the deep third reef in the main. He remembered the maxim drummed into them by their sailing instructor – if you think it's time to shake out a reef, wait 10 minutes, if you think it's time to reef, do it now.

What would you do?

It's a common dilemma. Closing the coast in rough weather, should you go for speed and reduce the time exposed to danger, or concentrate on making the boat as safe as possible and ride out the gale?

The boat is under pretty good control, well within the limits she can cope with and while the forecast is for possible gale force winds in 12 hours or more she is, at the present speed, just four hours from safety.

Traditional seamanship does indeed teach that it is better to reef too early rather than risk having to struggle in strong winds and rough seas to shorten sail. But that tradition developed in boats that were much heavier work to reef than the ones which most of us sail today.

If Dick and Margaret make a substantial sail reduction now they might well halve their speed, doubling the passage time to safety. They will then almost certainly be into a substantially stronger wind and the shallow entrance to Chichester will considerably magnify their problems.

I think this is an occasion for adopting the 'go for it' approach. In a couple of hours time there will be a weather shore under the Isle of Wight close to windward where it should be possible to find some modicum of shelter in which to set the storm jib. And on a reach, which they will have assuming that the wind doesn't veer or back unexpectedly, they could probably continue to make good progress under deep reefed main and motor if setting the storm jib turns out to be too difficult.

Q Nick's grip on the wheel tightened, his knuckles turning white. The log showed 14 knots as they surfed down the face of the wave. A burst of 14 knots under spinnaker while racing round the buoys on a sunny afternoon would have brought whoops of delight but under storm jib in South Biscay with over 40 knots of wind, large breaking waves and a grey and lowering sky it was just plain terrifying. What made it worse was that the wind and sea were still rising and it was only an hour before dusk. They still had 50 miles to go and the last shipping forecast had given no hint of the wind moderating in the next 24 hours.

Nick had learnt his sailing in high performance dinghies so planing in very marginal conditions was nothing new to him. Ted, the skipper, and the other two crew members were experienced offshore sailors but they would struggle at the helm with the boat surfing wildly and after two hours of steering he himself was starting to lose concentration.

'We can't go on like this,' Nick shouted to Ted. 'It's getting too dangerous, we'll have to find a way of slowing her down.'

The two of them were agreed that the high-speed dash could not continue but they were not unanimous on how best to keep the boat under control.

Ted favoured running on under bare poles but Nick didn't think that handing the storm jib would slow them down enough. He had tried it before in the same sort of conditions in a similar light displacement, beamy boat and they simply hadn't managed to reduce speed enough to bring her under control.

They also had to consider that it would be dark for the next 10 hours, so unless they could reduce speed to under four knots they would arrive on a lee shore in pitch blackness and probably 50 knots of wind. They needed good control to be certain that they made an accurate landfall at La Coruña, which would be possible to enter in almost any wind and sea conditions.

They hadn't enough long warps or a drogue on board to slow her down and

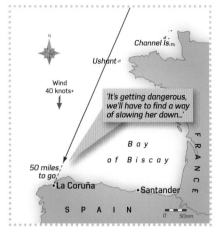

hold her stern to wind and sea. Reaching off under storm jib, Nick thought, could be a possibility but they might still be going too fast for safety. He favoured lying-to under bare poles with the helm lashed to leeward. That should be much less dangerous and with no need to steer they could conserve crew strength.

Ted was dubious. He had read depressing accounts of short-keeled boats like his being rolled over when left stopped and beam on to big waves. He preferred a tactic that would keep her moving through the water and preferably making ground towards the Spanish coast. In his view the shorter the time they spent at sea under survival conditions the better their chances of a happy outcome.

Has Nick or Ted got the best plan, or is there a better option, which neither of them has considered?

What would you do?

This is just about the worst possible nightmare for the skipper of a light displacement, short keeled, beamy boat. There are indeed plenty of recorded instances of them getting into bad trouble both sailing too fast and lying a-hull in very large seas.

Caught out in really unpleasant sea conditions is always going to put pressure on the skipper to find shelter as quickly as possible but closing a lee shore in wild weather has probably been the most common cause of loss of ships and seamen over the centuries. Better electronic navigation systems, reliable engines and more weatherly boats have removed some of the terrors of lee shores but they haven't totally eliminated them.

The traditional tactic of lying a hull was certainly favoured by the skippers of long keel heavy displacement working boats and yachts, for whom it reportedly worked well but it does seem to be much less effective for the modern lightweight high topside hull forms of modern yachts.

The only tactic that seems to have an unblemished record of success in light displacement hulls is putting the boat close hauled and sailing to windward, as slowly as possible, under storm jib. Whether this is because very few people have tried it and those that have are exceptionally good sailors – it is only possible if you have good heavy weather sails that are small enough to allow you to make to windward in very strong wind without being knocked flat and a reasonable supply of competent helmsmen – or because it really does work better than any other tactic is hard to tell. It is certainly counter-intuitive to expect a boat to go to windward under headsail alone in heavy weather but in fact most modern designs seem to do it quite well. It is the least risky option so it would certainly be worth a try.

Q When the tanker appeared, broad on the port bow, Jake knew that his run of good luck was about to end. He had enjoyed a superb sail under spinnaker, covering the 30 miles from his homeport to the start of the shipping lanes in a little over four hours. As he bore away, turning 15 degrees to port onto a dead run to cross the lanes at right angles, there wasn't a westbound ship in sight up to the east. He needed his luck to hold because they had set out later than planned and were only just going to make it to their destination in time for a daylight entrance.

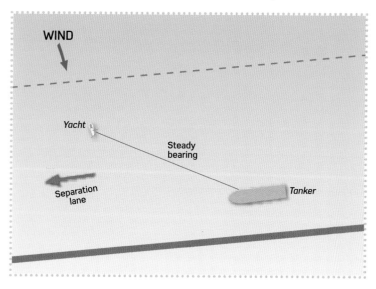

But now, well into the lane, he had been watching the tanker for some 10 minutes and there was no sign of a change of bearing. He hated this situation. He had no idea whether the tanker's watchkeeper would expect the sailing yacht to alter course so as not to impede the passage of a large ship in the lane or whether, in the developing situation in which there was clearly a risk of collision, the tanker would take action as a power driven vessel to keep out of the way of a sailing vessel.

Jake considered his options. If he altered course to port to pass astern of the tanker it would mean gybing the spinnaker, a somewhat fraught exercise in 18 knots of wind with just two of them on board, and the tanker might choose the exact same moment to alter course to starboard, thereby cancelling the effectiveness of the yacht's turn to port. Alternatively, he could alter course 20 degrees to starboard which would increase the apparent wind, bring his speed up by a couple of knots and he should easily pass clear ahead of the tanker. He would just have to be careful not to overdo the turn to starboard and risk a broach. He was keen to avoid having to drop the spinnaker because by the time they had re-packed it and sorted out the gear for re-hoisting they would have built in a delay of at least half an hour that could mean they arrived in darkness.

With the tanker an estimated two miles away he had just decided to go for the gybe and turn to port when his partner, Sarah, who had also been keeping a close eye on the developing situation, came up with an alternative. 'Why not collapse the spinnaker behind the main. That should slow us down enough to let her pass well ahead,' she suggested.

It's time for action.

What would you do?

My preferred solution used to be the same as Sarah's, collapse the spinnaker behind the main to slow down and allow the tanker to pass clear ahead. It has worked for me several times in the past but the last time it went badly wrong. It avoided the collision but it also resulted in a monumental spinnaker wrap around the forestay, which left us unmanoeuvrable and feeling highly vulnerable for the half-hour it took to sort out the wrap. A temporary deliberate spinnaker collapse is fine as long as it is short duration and there is no sea or swell but otherwise forget it.

Both of Jake's options seem seriously flawed. A turn to port for a ship approaching from the port side is always a risk, for the reason that Jake worked out for himself. The turn to starboard to increase speed might well result in passing clear ahead of the tanker but would you really want to? A temporary lull in the wind would slow you down and leave you straight in her path, a gust could lay you flat and at the mercy of the oncoming monster. Neither bears thinking about.

This situation is always going to be a difficult one because, as the skipper of the yacht, you can never be certain what the approaching ship is going to do. In this specific instance, carrying a spinnaker close to the upper limit of wind speed, it has too many possible traps to allow the complications to develop. Drop the spinnaker, harden up to put the tanker astern and let her pass. You may well have to arrive at your destination in the dark but at least you will be alive and your boat intact.

For those who like to consider the niceties of the regulations, the distinctions between 'shall not impede' and 'shall keep out of the way of' should give them plenty of food for thought. Whatever conclusion you reach, do remember how immense the bow of an oncoming tanker looks from the cockpit of your boat.

Q Ted had sailed onto the visitor's mooring the previous afternoon, hoping that the chandlery in the village might have an engine cooling water pump impeller to replace the one that had failed earlier in the day. He was out of luck, the so-called chandlery turned out to be more of a buckets and spades shop and all attempts to track down the local marine engineer had proved futile. By the time Ted got back on board it was too late to make the nearest harbour of any size before dark, so rather than attempt to make an engineless night passage he decided to stay until morning, a decision welcomed by the crew since it included a run ashore to the pub that provided the visitors' moorings.

The moorings had been relatively empty when Ted had arrived so picking one up under sail had been easy. During the evening, however, many more visitors had arrived and when Ted came to leave the following morning the little bay seemed crowded, with every buoy occupied with all the boats lying head to the wind, a brisk westerly blowing 20-25 knots. There was little more than a boat length between Ted and his neighbours on either side and a similar distance between his row and those ahead and astern.

A breakfast conference with the crew produced a number of suggestions for getting under way, some more helpful than others. They included running the engine for just long enough to get clear and hope to clear the moorings and shut it down

before it overheated. The dinghy sailor in the crew thought that hoisting a reefed main and backing it would allow them to make a sternboard passage between the boats to the east and out into open water. The favourite was simply to hoist both sails, back the jib with the main well eased so that the boat paid off onto a broad reach before she gathered way and sail under the stern of their neighbour on the port side, then pass between the southeastern-most boat on the moorings and the east cardinal beacon on the end of the rocks. A minority view was that they might not be able to bear away far enough to clear the stern of their neighbour so they should be ready to harden in the sheets and pass ahead of her.

Ted listened politely to his crew's suggestions. Ideally, he would wait a couple of hours, by which time a number of his neighbours would have left leaving him much more room to manoeuvre, but he was keen to get under way. The wind was forecast to drop later in the day and he didn't want to be left becalmed without an engine.

It's decision time.

What would you do?

As with many questions of seamanship, this one would never have arisen if the skipper had shown a little forethought and carried a more comprehensive set of engine spares.

All the suggestions from Ted's crew carry an unnecessary element of risk and we can all spot what they are in each case.

A safer solution would be to swing the boat on her mooring, taking care not to let her sheer across into one of her neighbours in the process, so that she lies stern to wind with the mooring ready to slip. No doubt she will lie less steadily that way round so the next stage of the manoeuvre needs good timing. When she is pointing for the middle of the gap between the boats to the east, unfurl a little genoa, slip the mooring and sail away. She should have steerage way very quickly but with only a little sail set she should not be accelerating dangerously fast. There is an inevitable risk that the boats on moorings will swing the wrong way at the wrong moment so fenders rigged on both sides would be a wise precaution.

The advantage of this departure plan over most of the crew's suggestions is that they involve risks of loss of control as the boat accelerates, leading to end-on collision or a rig tangle that would do substantial damage. The uncooled engine run is an idea which I suspect might work, with the impeller already gone the primary risk of damage is removed and most engines seem to take a while to come up to temperature but if it did go wrong it would do so expensively and I wouldn't have the nerve to put it to the test.

The downwind departure accepts that there may be contact with another boat but it will not be more than a slight brush and as long as there is no tangling of rigs or guardrails, which are unlikely on a dead run with the boat upright, it gives the best chance of avoiding damage.

A FAST ENCOUNTER?

 The forecast had promised light winds and a calm sea for the 60-mile northbound trip home across the shipping lanes. But it hadn't promised quite such poor visibility.

They had sailed at dawn and had been motoring through the flat calm for about six hours now. The last two had been pretty hectic for Don. With visibility down to something like a mile he had been glued to the radar screen checking the closest points of approach of the steady stream of traffic in the shipping lanes. At last he was beginning to feel that he could relax, the last three ships in the westbound lane had passed well astern and the screen was now clear up to the east.

He passed the good news up to the watch on deck and moved across from the chart table to the galley and put the kettle on to make coffee. He glanced back at the radar screen and noticed a new contact, fine on the starboard bow, at a range of six miles. He continued with the coffee making and when he next looked across at the radar, some two minutes later, the contact on the starboard bow had closed to 4.5miles. He switched off the gas under the kettle and gave his full attention to the radar screen.

The contact was very fine on the starboard bow, closing fast with just a hint of a change of bearing to the right and by the time he had worked out a closest point of approach, two cables down the starboard side, she was just over two miles away. In the last two minutes she had closed by one and a half miles. Their own speed was five knots and Don did some quick mental arithmetic, trying to work out the contact's speed, at the same time as he bounded up the companionway into the cockpit to see if there was anything visible fine on the starboard bow.

He could see nothing but the haze all round and Chris, at the helm, who had been listening closely to his running commentary on the rapidly approaching contact asked 'Do you want me to go to port to open up the miss distance, skipper?'

Before Don could answer, his other crewman, Nick, chipped in 'Surely not. This is an end-on encounter, we must go 90 degrees to starboard and we need to do it immediately.' Don stared into the mist ahead. He had seconds to make a decision.

What would you do?

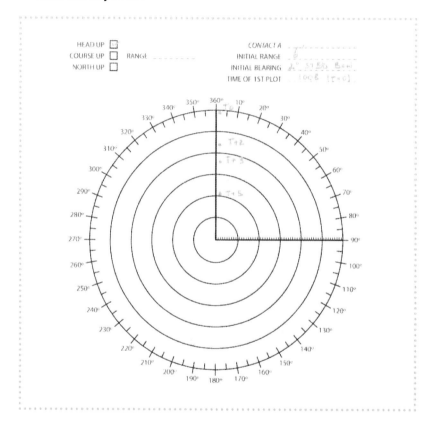

The relative speed of closing is 45 knots, fairly typical of an end on encounter with a high speed ferry. If Don has never given any thought to what he might do in this sort of situation he is unlikely to work out the best solution in a little under three minutes which is about the time to impact if he gets it wrong.

The only saving grace is that his best course of action is to make no manoeuvre until he sees the approaching vessel. At his present speed of five knots a turn to starboard with, by the time he has made it, some two minutes to impact will give him the opportunity to transfer just about two cables to starboard of his present track, in other words directly into the path of the approaching ship.

A turn to port would be a direct contravention of Rule 19, which governs the action to be taken when he detects another vessel by radar alone. This Rule requires him to determine if a close quarters situation is developing or a risk of collision exists, which he has done and arrived at the answer that a close quarters situation is developing but risk of collision does not (quite) exist. Since a close quarters situation is developing the Rule says that he must take avoiding action in ample time, which he can't, and that he must avoid an alteration of course to port for a vessel forward of the beam.

Onboard the approaching vessel the watch keeping officer is likely to be aware of Don's presence and by the time the range has closed to two miles he should have a pretty good idea of the likely passing distance. If he is satisfied that he is missing by a safe distance he will do nothing, if he thinks there is a risk of collision he will, or at least should, alter course to starboard. If he is about to take the latter course of action an alteration to port by Don could be fatal.

Don needs to keep a very close visual watch for the approaching vessel. She is likely to appear just over a minute before the two of them pass or collide. Once he has visual contact and can assess the aspect of the approaching speedster he will be in a much better position to take any avoiding action and at that stage he may need to act fast.

A number of secondary questions arise from this scenario. Is the approaching vessel proceeding at a safe speed? Probably not but it rather depends on the exact visibility and other factors such as the traffic density, and in any case the scenario is certainly not unlikely. Should Don have taken earlier action? In the circumstances, it is difficult to see how he could have made a much earlier assessment of the situation so he probably could not have done much more.

What he should, perhaps, have done, as soon as he came up into the cockpit, was to send Nick below to watch the radar and report on the contact's progress, refining the estimate of its closest point of approach but that is just a detail, he certainly needs to be in the cockpit himself to take an instant decision as soon as the ship becomes visible.

A BETTER IDEA?

26

Q It was nearing the end of David's first week as a professional Yachtmaster Instructor and by and large it had gone well. The previous evening morale had taken a bit of a dive, with the weather turning very cold but his decision to run the central heating for three hours had restored both the temperature and the spirits of his student crew. They had even seemed cheerful when he woke them at 0530 so they could make it back to base in time for the next student crew.

His feeling of general wellbeing was short lived. The skipper for the day had briefed the crew on his plan for leaving the berth and gone to start the engine, to be met by a refusal by the starter motor to produce more than a single revolution. David's investigation quickly revealed the source of the problem, the battery change over switch, instead of connecting only the domestic battery had been left in the 'Both' position the previous evening so the heater, which was always heavy on amps, had drained both the domestic and engine start batteries.

Having realised that it was going to be an engine-free day David decided

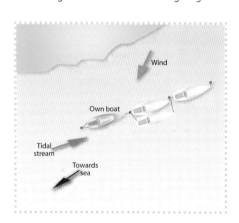

that there was no reason to sacrifice teaching time and invited his student skipper to revise his departure plan to cope with their altered circumstances. The diagram shows how the boat was berthed on the visitors' piles, with about a knot of upriver stream from astern and a fitful five knots of breeze from 45 degrees on the port bow.

The student's plan was simple.

He intended to rig both head and stern lines as slips and hoist main and headsail. Next he would back the headsail to port to push the bows to starboard, let go forward and aft and sail clear of the mooring before bearing away and gybing to turn towards the sea. He briefed his crew and asked for any questions.

Three of them simply nodded but the fourth, a youngster who had become something of a pain with his constant interruptions of 'I've got a better idea' throughout the week ran true to form and suggested that it would really be much better to turn the boat in her berth so that they could sail off with the wind on the quarter. There was a barely audible groan from the silent majority.

Put yourself in David's position.

What would you do?

Unfortunately, the pain is quite right, he really does have a better idea.

The problem with the student skipper's plan is that the wind is too light and the flood stream too strong for it to work. At her mooring the boat is effectively going backwards through the water at one knot so she has to accelerate to more than a knot over the ground before she has any steerage way. Even slipping the headrope first and backing the headsail to port will probably not push the bows far enough to starboard to allow a safe departure without risk of scraping along the starboard side of the outboard of the two boats berthed on the piles ahead.

The pain's plan has the advantage that once the boat is facing the other way it will be possible to hoist the headsail, sheet it and confirm that the boat will actually make headway over the tide before slipping either line and she has steerage way even while she is still in her berth. There is some risk, albeit a small one, that, in the process of turning the boat in her berth, the crew will lose control and allow her to hit the pile downtide as she swings to the tide but it's a fairly remote risk.

Q When Peter decided to sail single-handed on the return from St Peter Port on the island of Guernsey to his home port of Gorey on Jersey, he thought that the 30 mile trip, which he had made many times before, would be no problem.

And it wouldn't have been a problem, if the fuel berth had not been blocked by a large motor yacht with engine failure for three hours and the forecast southwesterly 3-4 hadn't turned into a southeasterly 4-5 and his hand held GPS hadn't decided to give up the ghost just as the weather started to deteriorate.

So it was that he found himself approaching the northwest corner of Guernsey in pitch darkness, visibility he guessed to be 3-4 miles, close hauled on starboard tack, peering into the wind, searching for the light on Grosnez Point. Just as he had decided that if he did not pick up the light in the next five minutes he would have to stand off and wait for daylight he sighted it, very fine on the starboard bow. He checked the characteristic and took a bearing, 102 degrees (T). He glanced down at the steering compass, it confirmed that his course steered was 100 degrees (T). That looked good, he knew from long experience that he would be making almost exactly 10 degrees of leeway so his course was probably about right.

Relieved at having made a landfall he took the waterproof chart out of the cockpit cave locker and switched on the torch to confirm the layout of the dangers. He needed to pass at least half a mile to seaward of the lighthouse to clear Plemont point which lay to the east-northeast of it but no more than 1.5 miles off to clear south of the Paternosters. Looking at the light he guessed that he should pass between half a mile and a mile to seaward of it. Grosnez was the only light visible. Once he picked up Sorel Point he could use its white sector as a safe clearing bearing and shortly after that it would be daylight. For the time being, however, he had only Grosnez to go by and his only instruments other than the compass were a log and echo sounder, both of which he knew were pretty accurate. Chartwork would be almost impossible in the prevailing conditions, she wouldn't steer herself for long enough for him to plot courses and bearings with any accuracy.

Peter considered his options. Heaving to and waiting for daylight had attractions but the weather was getting steadily worse and hanging around for a couple of hours didn't seem like a clever idea. These were his home waters, he knew them well. He thought through his navigational plan and settled down to getting the best out of the boat. At least he didn't have to grapple with tidal sets, it was just approaching slack water.

How is he going to navigate accurately enough to find the safe water between the Jersey and the Paternosters?

What would you do?

A One way in which Peter could navigate through the passage between Plemont and the Paternosters would be by using a special case of the running fix for which no plotting is needed, the so called 'Beam and four point bearing'.

The way it works is to take the log reading when the fixing mark, in this case Grosnez light, is four points (45 degrees) off the starboard bow. The bearing has to be relative to the course made good, not the course steered, so the light would be on an actual bearing of 135 degrees (T). Sail on and again note the log reading when the light is exactly on the starboard beam, ie bearing 180 degrees (T). At this point the distance off the light is the same as the distance run between the two log readings.

When the lighthouse is abeam Peter knows his distance off. If he is too far off the light he can tack and sail directly towards it for the distance which he needs to give a safe clearance off the Paternosters. Similarly, if he is too close to it he can sail directly away for the distance needed to clear Plemont point.

Relying on a single navigational reference point would, of course, carry a degree of risk. Keeping an eye on the depth by echo sounder could help to minimise it, although not by much since the dangers on both sides are very steep-to. A good visual lookout, for breakers on the Paternosters or the shadowy outline of Jersey would probably be a better check that the primary method of navigation had not gone badly wrong.

MEDITERRA-NEAN MOOR

28

Q It was Jerry's first taste of Mediterranean cruising and it had all happened rather quickly. A really lousy long range forecast the day before the summer holiday cruise had come close to sparking a mutiny. The children had whined all evening about the miseries of seasickness, cold bunks, walks in the rain and the fun that all their school friends would be having on sunny south European beaches. So Jerry had logged on to the internet and searched for Med sailing holidays. He was rewarded by a special offer last minute deal for a fortnight's charter of a 40 footer in the Ionian. He phoned the number and 48 hours later they were sailing across a sea which, if not wine dark, was at least sunlit, his own boat lying deserted but well secured to her mooring on the rain lashed south coast of England.

Entering a Mediterranean harbour for the first time Jerry looked at the berthing options. There were a couple of dozen yachts, a few locals but mainly flotilla boats by the look of them, berthed bows to the quay with anchors out astern, leaving just a couple of spare slots. The little harbour was well sheltered from the northwesterly afternoon breeze so getting into the berth should not present any problems but Jerry was not keen to berth bows to the quay like everyone else. Stern to seemed to him to be a better option.

His crew, while enthusiastic, were not particularly strong so there was much to recommend using the bower anchor with its associated electric windlass on the bow, the kedge on the stern would have to be weighed by hand when it came to leaving time. He also wondered if stern to would be better during the night when the land breeze filled in from the NE, straight onto the quay, as he had read that it was prone to do. There was enough fetch for quite a chop to build up and he wanted everyone to have a good night's sleep, undisturbed by the loud lapping of waves under the shallow slope of the counter.

The sailing directions were little help, they mentioned plans for a new quay to replace the old one, which was said to be in a bad state of repair and it was clearly the new quay that he was looking at.

Should he have the courage of his convictions and risk being the only skipper to moor stern to?

What would you do?

Jerry's reasons for wanting to go stern on to the quay are sensible but the fact that nobody else has done so must have some significance. It could be that the flotilla boats are in their first harbour of the fortnight and the lead boat crew thought it would be easier to get them all in going forwards and it might be that the quay is much frequented by land-based holiday makers so the boats already berthed think that the better privacy afforded by a bows to mooring is an overriding consideration. It is also possible, however, that those already berthed know that bows to is the only safe way, because when the new quay was built the contractors were none too fussy about removing the underwater remains of the old one. If this is the case then the consequences of a stern to berthing would be, at best an unbridgeable gap between boat and quay or at worst a badly damaged rudder.

Without a recce in the dinghy, which could be an unwarranted complication, Jerry would probably be wiser not to take the risk of being 'the only man in step'.

29

RADAR MAKES LIFE EASIER?

Q Last season Ben would not have sailed in these conditions, the forecast of possible fog would have been enough for him to cancel the long weekend trip to France in favour of pottering around Poole harbour. But the visibility had been no worse than moderate when they left the harbour, the Force 4 westerly had been the ideal wind and the fog was only 'possible at first' so the passage to Cherbourg had seemed a reasonable bet, particularly since the newly installed radar seemed to be working well.

At midnight, approaching the shipping lanes, with a halo of mist around the masthead light indicating much reduced visibility, the first shipping contact of the westbound lane appeared, at a range of six miles, 80 degrees on the port bow. Ben briefed the watch on deck to keep a good lookout and settled down to keep track of the approaching contact. It took a little under 10 minutes to close to three miles and, as far as he could tell with the boat yawing up to 10 degrees, there was no appreciable change of bearing. Ben nipped up into the cockpit. They were making six knots, with the wind on the starboard beam. He briefed the helmsman on the progress of the approaching contact, asked him to steer as steady a course as possible, made a mental note that they could turn no more than 45 degrees to starboard without tacking and returned to the chart table and the radar screen.

Three minutes later the range had closed to two miles, bearing still showing no discernable movement. He reckoned that he must be quite fine on the starboard bow of the approaching vessel. According to the rules it was up to her to keep clear, but she was probably huge and judging by the rate at which the range was closing she was doing something like 20 knots. Having right of way meant little if she was not going to alter course.

Another three minutes passed, the range was down to one mile and still the bearing showed no real change. There was still no sign of any lights on the bearing of the contact and no fog signal had been heard.

Time's running out.

What would you do?

Aen has made the false assumption that the approaching contact is the 'give way' vessel. In fact the rules that govern which vessel should give way, Section II of the steering and sailing rules, only apply to vessels in sight of each other. He is, however, correct in his assumption that the contact is going quite fast, probably about 19 knots and that he is about 20 degrees on her starboard bow.

Ben has ascertained that a close quarters situation is developing but, if he is using a ship's head up unstabilised radar, it is difficult to be certain whether or not he is actually on a collision course. The Officer of the Watch on the other ship is likely to have a more sophisticated radar, with ARPA, which will be telling him either that he is on a collision course or, if not, what the closest point of approach is likely to be – always assuming that Ben has an effective radar reflector and has been detected on the other ship's radar.

The rule that advises on manoeuvring in this situation is 19(d), which says 'A vessel which detects by radar alone the presence of another vessel shall determine if a close quarters situation is developing and/or risk of collision exists. If so, she shall take avoiding action in ample time, provided that when such action consists of an alteration of course, so far as possible the following shall be avoided:

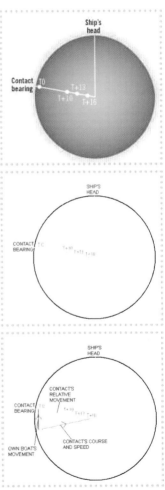

(i) an alteration of course to port for a vessel forward of the beam, other than for a vessel being overtaken.

(ii) an alteration of course towards a vessel abeam or abaft the beam.'

The imponderables, as far as Ben is concerned are whether or not he has been detected by the other vessel, whether or not her watchkeeper has decided that he needs to alter course as required by Rule 19 and, if so, what alteration he should make. If the other vessel is going to alter course and comply with Rule 19 she is likely to turn to starboard, to pass Ben down her port side.

Ben can't just do nothing, he has to take positive action to avoid a collision. His least unfavourable option is to tack, putting the other vessel fine on his starboard quarter. This will have the double advantages of reducing the closing rate and presenting a smaller target. But it will make matters worse if the other vessel alters course to starboard, so it would certainly be a good idea for Ben to start his engine and roll up his genoa so that he has full freedom of manoeuvre and continue to keep a very close watch on the radar. Once the engine is running he may need to turn directly away from the approaching contact, which he could not do under sail alone.

Does radar really make life easier? Probably not but if used intelligently it may well make it longer.

A FORCED PASSAGE?

As he left the pub, Grant was amazed to find how much the weather had changed in just two hours. It had been blowing a gentle southerly when he went in for dinner, it was now a fresh easterly.

The dinghy trip back to the boat was decidedly bouncy, Bray Harbourin Alderney was not particularly well sheltered from the east and completely open to the northeast. Once on board Grant headed for the chart table and the Navtex receiver. The coastal waters forecast, which had been predicting strengthening southwesterly winds earlier that day was now suggesting strong to gale force north easterlies. The depression which had been expected to move northeast must be deepening and moving southeast into France. A glance at the anemometer showed a wind speed of 25 knots and the barometer had fallen six millibars since mid-afternoon.

Grant realised that staying in Alderney and riding out the gale would not be a good plan. The wind had backed 15 degrees since he left the shore and it was increasing rapidly. He had about an hour's daylight left. Grant's crew, his two teenage sons were good sailors but they had spent the previous night at sea on passage from Chichester and they were looking forward to a good night's sleep. Much of the passage from Chichester had been under power and the diesel remaining in the tank could not be guaranteed to last for more than a couple of hours.

Grant quickly ruled out a downwind dash to Guernsey because of the likelihood of dangerous sea conditions firstly in the Swinge, then in Little Russell, with gale-force wind against tide. He also dismissed the idea of heading back to UK or putting to sea and riding out the worst of the weather because of his limited crew strength. He would, he decided, make for Cherbourg, just 23 miles away, around a headland. It would undoubtedly be a bumpy passage but he should be able to make it in little more than five hours, the entry was straightforward even in the worst of sea conditions and it should

76

just be getting light as they arrived.

For the first couple of hours they made good progress. Then off Cap de la Hague the wind strengthened to 45 knots in the gusts and with the storm jib and triple reefed main they were being blown flat, losing control and rounding up head to wind. They were out of control and going sideways as quickly as they were going forwards so clearly had to shorten sail, which meant handing either the main or the storm jib. Grant knew that this was going to be an important decision. He was already tired, lowering either sail was going to be hard work and if he got it wrong he probably would not have the strength to re-hoist the sail he had just lowered and hand the other one.

What would you do?

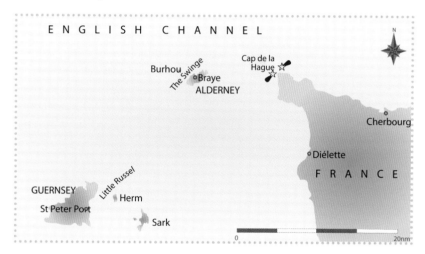

Grant is probably having to cope with wind strengths which he has never previously encountered, so he can't just do what worked last time. Provided that his boat has no particularly quirky handling characteristics he will probably be better off with just the jib. It will be easier to stow the main, working by the mast, than to have to claw down the storm jib right forward and, as a broad generalisation, modern boats go to windward better under just a headsail than under the main alone.

If you have experience of these conditions in your own boat and you know that she is one of the minority which behaves better under main alone then your advice is, of course, likely to be different.

THROW CAUTION TO THE WIND?

Q Henry cursed the weather forecasters. When he set out from Poole for the 64-mile passage to Cherbourg at midday they had promised a westerly Force 4-5, later backing southerly and increasing 6-7, locally gale 8.

He knew that in weather forecasts the word later had a very specific meaning, more than 12 hours, so he had reckoned on at least 12 hours of broad to beam reach at over six knots, which should see him safely alongside in Cherbourg at least two hours before the wind headed and increased. At 2000, 10 hours out, the wind had gone just south of east and was gusting up to 45 knots, Force 9 in his book. He had shortened sail to a triple-reefed main and just a corner of rolled genoa. His speed was down to three knots and he was still 18 miles dead downwind from Cherbourg.

He huddled into the forward end of the cockpit, wishing a hideous fate on all weather forecasters and considering his options. He knew that he would make very little progress to windward in the prevailing conditions under engine. Under sail, laying no better than 50 degrees off the wind, it would take at least nine hours to reach Cherbourg. Two of his three crew had already succumbed to seasickness and taken to their bunks and he wasn't feeling too good himself. It was bitterly cold on deck and it could only get worse when darkness fell in two hour's time. His home port of Poole was just 42 miles dead to leeward. If he bore away he could drop the main, unroll half of the genoa and make 8-10 knots in this strength of wind, giving a passage time to Poole of something in the region of five hours.

Unfortunately, he had been busy reefing at 1754 and missed the Shipping Forecast so he had no idea what the forecasters thought that the wind would do next – not that he would put much faith in whatever they predicted! His train of thought was broken by a shout from Mike at the helm, calling for him to take over. He did so, just in time to allow Mike to dive for the leeward rail where he was miserably sick.

Henry knew that he was virtually singlehanded. Should he go for the longer but potentially faster passage back to Poole or keep plugging to windward towards Cherbourg?

What would you do?

No doubt there are many who think that the right answer to this question is that Henry should never have got himself into this pickle in the first place. Setting out on a 64-mile passage in the face of a forecast gale with a crew who are prone to seasickness was not clever. He is quite right about the definition of 'later' but quite wrong to expect such precision in forecasts. He is also too precise in his expectation of the wind strength in a Force 8, which, while defined as a mean wind speed of 34-40 knots is always likely to include stronger gusts.

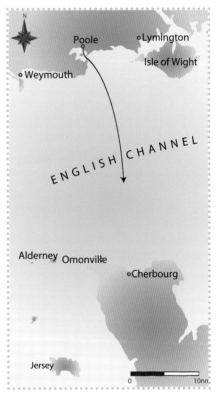

One may assume that since he is persevering with a tiny corner of unfurled genoa he does not have a storm jib, further reason not to set out in such forecast conditions.

However, Henry is in a mess and never mind how he got there, he has an important decision to make. The downwind sleigh ride back to Poole certainly has attractions. Henry must be getting tired and the less time he has to spend at sea now the better. The sailing will be exhilarating and going downwind should be much warmer and drier than plugging to windward but the downwind ride carries a number of dangers.

The longer the wind blows from the south the rougher the sea will become. As it builds, the steering will become more difficult and there will be an increasing risk of a heavy broach, with possible damage to rig and hull. If he makes it that far, a downwind entry into Poole in an onshore gale in pitch darkness with an exhausted helmsman at 0200 will be extremely hazardous.

The slog to windward to Cherbourg has few immediate attractions but at least it should be the safer option. Any shift in the wind will help and as he slowly closes the French coast he should benefit from the shelter of the weather shore, giving smoother water and faster progress. He might also do better to roll the genoa right away and continue under main and engine. The small amount of genoa he is using at present is probably producing more drag than drive and while the engine on its own may not give much speed the combination of reefed main and engine could be much more effective, allowing him to point higher and make slightly more speed through the water. (Just one caution on this, some engines don't like being run at large angles of heel and if this is the case with Henry's he will just have to stick with his inefficient genoa).

The prospect of continuing to windward may look bleak but if he perseveres conditions should improve and with luck one of his crew should recover to give him a spell on the helm as the sea flattens out under the shelter of the land.

BACK TO BASICS?

Q George switched to Channel 79 on the VHF and waited for the 1603 weather broadcast from Ile de Batz. It promised haze and fog overnight. He would have to be prepared for a difficult approach to Morlaix later that evening.

'Thank goodness for the GPS chart plotter,' he thought. When he first started to use it he had been reluctant to trust it but it had never let him down so that increasingly he had come to rely on it. On this particular passage, along the rock-fringed north Brittany coast to the east of L'Aberwrach, with only a succession of seemingly identical water towers, church steeples and radio masts some 5 miles away available as fixing marks, he was particularly grateful for its reassuring presence above the chart table.

He turned to look at it and was surprised to find the screen blank. He had used it to check on the pilotage out of L'Aberwrach that morning and glanced at it to confirm they were on track several times since. He couldn't think why any of the crew should have switched it off. He pressed the ON button and to his dismay nothing happened. All the other instruments were working perfectly. Five minutes later the test meter had confirmed the power supply to the plotter was good, so the problem had to be internal. George knew all about modern electronics – he knew if they didnt work, he couldn't fix them.

George dug out the paper chart, hand bearing compass, dividers, plotter and the paraphernalia of visual navigation. The log was not much help in establishing a position, it recorded the time of departure from L'Aberwrach some four hours previously and he was aware that they had been making between 4 and 5 knots in the light northwesterly breeze ever since. That gave him an approximate position, accurate to within about four miles. Peering through the binoculars at the land he could see two water towers, several church spires and a tall radio mast but the haze was already starting to build. A series of bearings made little sense, except that the two water towers gave position lines which crossed right on his guessed position. Another fix half an hour later, on the same two water towers, tied in exactly with the accurately worked up EP from the earlier fix. 'Good,' thought George, 'I haven't lost my touch with traditional navigation.'

He reconsidered his planned track, through the Canal de Batz and on to Morlaix. He felt confident about pressing on, he should sight Ile de Batz, currently some 10 miles away, within the next half hour and if the fog came in earlier than expected he could always anchor in the lee of Batz and wait for the fog to clear in the morning.

Is he getting over-confident?

What would you do?

George has just made the most dangerous mistake possible, he has situated his appreciation rather than appreciated his situation. Navigation information which does not tie in with the assumed position is always unwelcome; George is likely to ignore warnings of danger just because they are unpalatable.

George may of course be right but he needs more supporting evidence. GPS is so reliable and accurate that it is easy to forget the basic precept of visual navigation, which calls for a truly self-checking procedure, albeit less accurate than a GPS position. The important point about all navigation is not so much its accuracy as its reliability and hence the advice to include three bearings in all visual fixes – they are no more accurate than two bearing fixes but they are likely to show when an error or false identification has been made. No doubt some will feel that with George's total reliance on his GPS and chart plotter, with no visual navigation back-up or even a record in the log, he deserves all the trouble in which he finds

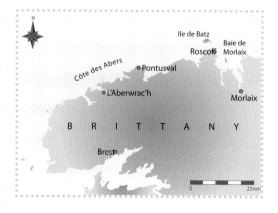

himself, but however unwise he may have been I suspect that his faith in electronics is not untypical of amateur and professional navigators.

Q John had been nervous about berthing in Ploumanac'h. Friends at the club had said that the spectacular pink granite in the area made a visit well worthwhile. They had also warned him about the difficulty of securing to the visitors' moorings there, the French equivalent of pile moorings, with the piles replaced by buoys and floating dumbbell fenders between them. The problem, he had been told, was that the whole mooring lacked any sort of rigidity and the lines which secured the dumbbells at each end were prone to fouling propellers.

In the event, berthing had been simple, as there was another British boat on the other side of the dumbbell and her crew had taken his lines so that he was able to secure to her and then take head and stern lines to the buoys in the dinghy.

Now it was time to leave and John would have to cope on his own, his friendly neighbour having left the previous evening. He was lying with the wind, a moderate breeze, very fine on the starboard bow, blowing him onto the dumbbell on his port side. He had about three boat lengths of clear water on his starboard side before the obstruction of another trot of fore and aft moorings and the channel to the harbour exit was some 45 degrees on his starboard bow.

Ideally he would have liked to take a spring from his port quarter to the forward mooring buoy, go astern against it to swing his bow through the wind and motor away. That, however, would drag the head buoy aft and bring his prop dangerously close to the ground tackle for the stern mooring buoy and the line that ran from it to the dumbbell.

The alternative was to take a head spring to the stern buoy, go ahead on it to swing his stern out and then motor away astern. That would at least reduce the possibility of a fouled prop but his boat was always difficult to control going astern, with a very strong tendency for the bow to pay off rapidly until she had built up good sternway. He wasn't at all sure that he would have room to gather enough way to bring her under control.

John realised that his crew were waiting for him to give them his plan for departure.

What would you do?

It is difficult to see a simple plan for leaving the mooring under power, but why not sail away?

Set the main and a half-rolled genoa or working jib. Start the engine but leave it in neutral. Rig the stern spring to the forward mooring buoy, back the headsail to port (he may have to wait for a favourable shift) to push the bow through the wind and then sail out on port tack. As soon as the stern comes clear of the mooring, put the engine ahead, roll up the genoa and motor out.

RECKONING ON THE ROCKS?

34

Q Frank was pleased with his new boat. He had always dreamed of owning a long keel, heavy displacement ketch and her performance on the delivery trip from Harwich to Falmouth had lived up to his expectations. The four old sailing friends he had brought along as crew seemed equally impressed.

It had been a beat across the mouth of the Thames Estuary and a close reach all the way from Dover, with southerly or south-southwesterly winds between Force 4 and 6. As they moved west the sea and swell had built but the boat had never faltered, seeming progressively more and more at home as she approached the open Atlantic. The heavy 50 footer was certainly much more comfortable in these conditions than his old light displacement 35 footer.

Closing on St Anthony Head at the entrance to the Fal the wind began to head and drop. Frank hardened in the sheets and pointed up to give an offing from the point. Gradually the speed dropped as the swell became steeper and the wind more fitful. Frank handed over the helm to Richard and went below to start the engine. He turned the key, heard the starter motor engage, but the engine would not even turned over. He checked the battery switch; to his dismay he had been running with both engine start and domestic batteries connected there was no reserve.

Back in the cockpit the wind was now very light and speed had fallen to little more than one knot. She was still pointing clear to seaward of St Anthony Head but making a lot of leeway. The sheets were pinned in hard, there was nothing in reserve. He glanced at the breaking swell crashing on the rocks some 200 yards off the lee bow. The transit of the seaward edge of St Anthony Head seemed to be holding against Pendennis Castle on the far side of the Estuary. The sea ahead and to leeward looked glassy. Astern and to windward there were ripples, even white horses. The log was now reading under one knot and the noise of breakers growing louder. At least they had plenty of depth, the echo sounder showed 18 metres.

What would you do?

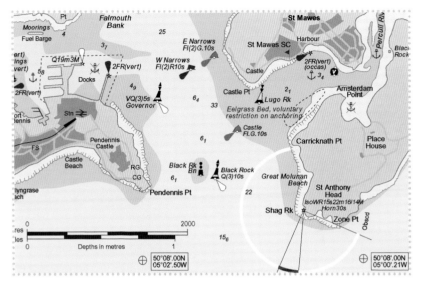

Frank is experiencing the relatively common phenomenon of an onshore wind going very light close under high ground. Although he is making little headway he needs to get clear of the coast or he will simply be washed ashore by the sea and swell. It is probably too deep to be certain of an anchor holding – although the anchor could be his last resort if all else fails – so he needs to do his best to sail clear.

If he continues on his present course he will almost certainly hit the rocks, as the wind continues to fail and the swell grows steeper close to the shore. Tacking would be risky, with the boat moving so slowly in a steep swell it is quite likely that she will miss stays and fall back onto the old tack with all steerage way lost. The best bet would be to bear away and gybe. It will seem horrific, pointing the boat towards the rocks but as long as the crew are sensible with the sheets, easing them gradually to keep as much drive as possible and making sure that the mizzen is not left pinned in, there should be very little risk of failure.

Q It had been a straightforward northbound passage, the wind a firm Force 4 from the East, good visibility for crossing the shipping lanes and GPS, as usual, had given continuous position and course and speed made good. The last 15 miles to Plymouth, however, looked as if they might be more challenging. The visibility had deteriorated very quickly, dropping from some 10 miles to just a few hundred yards.

Josh decided it would be prudent to post a lookout at the bows and get the whole crew into lifejackets and briefed to keep a good listening watch. He thought about his options for the entry into Plymouth Sound, which was not going to be easy in a yacht without radar. The entrance to the west of the breakwater was certainly the widest of the two but it was also the more heavily used by ships and fishing boats. The eastern one was much narrower and involved passing closer to dangers and while it was little used by large vessels it did carry a certain amount of yacht and fishing boat traffic. Whichever entrance he chose, once past the breakwater he would have to join the main channel at some point for the passage through the harbour to his mooring up a river.

He shared his thoughts with the rest of the crew, to see if they had any ideas on the best way to avoid close encounters in the poor visibility, which was now down to about 100 yards.

'We aren't in any hurry to be home, so why don't we anchor Cawsand for the night, it will probably be clearer in the morning,' said Dominic.

Josh wasn't too impressed, the bay was a lee shore in an easterly and the holding ground was not particularly good.

'Jennycliff Bay would be a better anchorage,' chimed in Nick. 'It's well sheltered under the cliffs there and if we went in through the eastern entrance we wouldn't really have to cross the main shipping channel. I know the holding there is no better than Cawsand but at least it should be calm.'

'Or we could go into the Yealm and anchor in Cellar's Bay,' suggested Frank.

'I know it's a narrow entrance but it will be well sheltered and there isn't likely to be much on the move in or out of the river in this visibility.'

Josh pondered Frank's idea. The navigable channel into the Yealm was only some 50 yards wide, had steep rocks either side and a sand bar to the north. Would the GPS be accurate enough to allow them to find the channel safely in visibility of 100 yards?

What would you do?

A Cawsand is a non-starter, a lee shore with a two and a half mile fetch in an easterly Force 4 and uncertain holding – not a good idea. The western entrance in 100 yards visibility has little appeal, the poor visibility will deter many from setting out from Plymouth but the possibility of collision cannot be ruled out so it should be avoided.

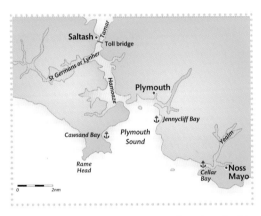

An approach through the eastern entrance to an anchorage in Jennycliff Bay reduces the chance of a collision but does not completely eliminate it, so that has to be a possibility.

The favourite, however, has to be the anchorage in Cellars Bay, just inside the Yealm. It is highly unlikely that any other boat of any size will be leaving the river so the possibility of collision is minimal. The pilotage should be within the capability of GPS, as long as it is taken slowly with a good visual lookout and a close eye on the echo sounder.

Q When planning their summer cruise Ian and Kate had agreed that a week should be ample time to make it from their home port to their destination 240 miles southwest, where their daughter, son-in-law and grandchildren could join them by air. They had reckoned without the four days of southwesterly gales that had kept them in their home port.

The wind had veered at last and they sailed early on the Thursday morning with a moderate northerly breeze, with 48 hours before their relatives flew in. They thought about heading for somewhere closer and hiring a car to embark their visitors but decided against it. The original aim of heading for the calmer seas and warmer weather further south where the children were likely to have a much more enjoyable holiday was, they decided, still achievable.

They made excellent progress, bowling along on an ever broadening reach as the wind continued to veer gradually into the northeast. Dusk found them entering the southwestbound shipping lane, just under halfway. By now they were on a dead run, with the genoa boomed out to windward and as the following sea built the autopilot was having more and more difficulty holding the course, with the boat yawing up to 20 degrees each way. This brought them close to collapsing the genoa on one side and to gybing the main on the other. It also made it difficult to work out the risk of collision with the increasing number of ships which they were encountering as they moved into the shipping lane.

Ian, who was standing watch from 2100 to midnight, put up with the unsatisfactory situation for an hour, before a wilder than usual yaw to port resulted in an accidental gybe. Kate, not yet in her bunk, came on deck to see what the noise was. They discussed the situation. At their present speed of six knots they had only about six hours in hand, so slowing down was not an option. They could hand steer but that would be tiring and difficult to keep track of the shipping situation with only one on watch. Running the engine would give the rudder more bite and perhaps help the autopilot to cope a little better. They had enough fuel to motor the whole way; it would be noisy and not particularly satisfying, but it would get the job done.

They also considered abandoning the plan to reach their intended destination by Saturday morning and heading for a closer port.

Put yourself in their place.

What would you do?

A dead run is never a happy course and neither is it sensible to cross a busy shipping lane at a narrow angle.

Their best bet would be to gybe onto a broad reach to the south, so that the sails fill without any need to goosewing, the steering is easier and the angle of crossing the shipping lane is much broader. Once well clear to the south of the shipping lanes they can gybe back again and broad reach to the west.

They will sail a little further by following this zig-zag route but they should also sail faster so the increase in time to their destination should be very small.

A DIFFICULT BERTH?

Q Don and Joan's first Channel crossing was almost complete. It had been much longer than they expected. When they set out heading due south the forecast had promised westerlies and a straightforward reach all the way from their home port, a passage time of about 15 hours. Halfway across the wind had backed and increased, giving them a cold wet beat. After 24 hours at sea their arrival off the breakwater came as a welcome relief.

They entered the marina just as the sun rose and the duty officer at the entrance directed them to the visitors' pontoons. The rain had cleared to a bright clear morning but the wind, now veered to the northwest, was still strong. Joan spotted the row of berths to which they had been directed. The

finger pontoons were very narrow compared to those they were used to and there were just three vacant berths, two either side of a finger and one at which there was a motor cruiser berthed on the other side of the finger.

Staring at the berths through the binoculars Joan noticed that there was nobody about to help with the lines and there didn't seem to be any cleats, just metal bars like flattened croquet hoops on which to secure warps. She also noticed that the warps from the motor cruiser to the finger pontoon seemed to be very tight. She pointed this out to Don, commenting that she did not much like the idea of lying in a berth adjacent to a boat whose warps would be bound to squeak whenever there was the slightest movement in the marina.

Joan thought that port side to on the empty finger looked like the best bet. Don disagreed and insisted that they berth at the finger with the motor cruiser on the other side of it.

'You are going to have to be quick getting onto the pontoon with the warps,' he told Joan. 'We will be dead head to wind in the berth so I'll have to make a fairly fast approach and it will be difficult to hold her stopped for long. Can you stand by the shrouds, outboard of the guardrails, with the head and stern warps in hand ready to jump as soon as you can reach the end of the pontoon, please.'

Has Don made the right decision?

What would you do?

Don certainly has made the right major decision. In this part of the world, the finger pontoons are so narrow that if you jump on the end of one it sinks a long way and unless you have the balance of a gymnast you are unlikely to stay on it. The motor cruiser with the tight warps will fulfil two useful functions: it will act as a guardrail on the far side of the narrow pontoon and its tight warps will stop the end of the pontoon from sinking when Joan jumps onto it.

One minor point, Joan would be better just to take the headrope ashore and concentrate on securing that. Once the bows are secure the stern isn't going anywhere and the other warps can be taken to the pontoon in slow time.